You Can Change Your Life

You Can Change Your Life

A Future Different from Your Past with the Hoffman Process

TIM LAURENCE

HODDER
MOBIUS

Hodder & Stoughton

First published in Great Britain in 2003 by Hodder and Stoughton
A division of Hodder Headline

1 3 5 7 9 10 8 6 4 2

A CIP catalogue record for this title is available from the British Library

Reference to the Hoffman Quadrinity Process®, methods and techniques is
made herein pursuant to the express authorisation of Hoffman Institute
International, which reserves all rights. Materials fully describing the Hoffman
Quadrinity Process, methods and techniques are available only through the
Hoffman Institute subject to disclosure agreements.

ISBN 0 340 82522 7

Typeset in Legacy Serif Book by
Palimpsest Book Production Limited,
Polmont, Stirlingshire
Printed and bound in Great Britain by
Clays Ltd, St Ives plc

Hodder and Stoughton
A division of Hodder Headline
338 Euston Road
London NW1 3BH

To my father Keith Laurence (1920–2001) and my brother Justin Laurence (1956–1993): you gave plenty of proof that life is for living fully.

Acknowledgements

I would like to express my appreciation to the many great people who have been behind this book. Firstly, my deep gratitude to Bob Hoffman for these teachings, which it is my privilege to pass on. In the same lineage, I am in debt to Hoffman teachers who lit the path: in the USA, Stanley Stefancic, Kani and Barbara Comstock; in Germany, Martin Kremer, Jochen and Christiane Windhausen; in France, Karen Reuter; in Brazil, Marisa Thame; in Australia, Volker Krohn; in Switzerland, Wolfgang Michael Harlacher and Claudia Coppetti; in Italy, Mike and Daniela Wenger; and in Spain, Luis Fernando Camara.

Over the years and especially since Bob Hoffman's death, I have been in deep admiration of Raz Ingrasci, who heads up the Hoffman Institute USA. Along with Marisa Thame of Sao Paolo, a fellow director of Hoffman International, I have had many enrichening discussions about the role of our work. Marisa's passing on leaves us all with a truly spiritual inspiration. Thanks for showing us how it could be done and for building an international community.

For the fact that there actually is a book, two couples – Seana McGee and Maurice Taylor in Sausalito (who asked the simple question, 'Have you ever thought about getting an agent?') and Mike Fishwick and Imogen Taylor in London, who explained that publishers were human beings too. Sue

Bowes demonstrated with enormous skill how to hack a path through the jungle of ideas and methods, and have a lot of laughs along the way. Julian Shuckburgh dropped some pearls of wisdom in the 'Is there anyone out there?' era.

In my own family background, I'm extremely lucky that my mother, a former journalist, loved writing and always encouraged me to sit down and do it. I'm also fortunate to have as a stepmother, Janet Laurence, prolific writer and patient supporter of those who have not been published, who was always there with advice and encouragement. For finding a publisher, thanks to my wonderful agent Laura Morris in London, whose commitment and enthusiasm were truly heartening. Susan Schulman in New York gave an immediate 'Yes' when hearing of the idea. Thanks to Rowena Webb and Emma Heyworth-Dunn of Hodder and Stoughton – for being all, or even more than, a person needs in a publisher. You taught me a lot without probably realising you were giving lessons!

For help in getting down to it: Alexander Gilbert who offered the perfect house in Cape Town at the perfect time and Ian Morgan for telling me to limit my hours of writing (four a day, max) so that I still got to see daylight and people.

Thanks to Paddy Welles and Paul Rebillot in years gone by for teaching me to think outside the box; Cynthia Merchant for her work on ritual, as well as her friendship when I left the US for my original home; Lois Evans, Amy Jenkins, Emma Amyatt-Leir, Patrick Holford, John Campbell and all those who have made our work find fertile ground. To the many students who have guided me on the path of compassion and shown me that by listening deeply truth emerges; your stories provide the ripe fruit on the tree.

My wonderful team in the UK carried on when I was elsewhere. On the teaching team I'd like to thank Karen Jepsen, Tom Currie, Lisa Wenger, Devi Razo and Ben Shuckburgh, plus their understanding partners who maintain their home life. In the office, thanks to Nikki Wyatt, who acted as an angel, deftly guiding us through all kinds of changes, Victoria 'Godsend' Godsall and Carolyn Brice. In Ireland, thanks must go to Rosemary Lennon Maher, Martina Breen Keenan and John O'Reilly who have always deeply cared for the healing work. In South Africa, Michelle Sparks. Beryleen Andrea in California, who has done so much for Hoffman International and always knows exactly where to find the information. And all the teachers from the other countries who fly over and give their energy despite jet lag and more – Anne, Cheshta, Craig, Ed, Ginger, Helen, Katrin, Linda H. and R, Loreen and Mark.

When we needed a home for our work, Michelle Stevenson showed not just vision but also a power to make it happen. Florence House is a remarkable place thanks to your work and connection with unseen sources.

But above all more thanks than can be said to my wife Serena, for creating a loving space within which I could simply sit and write – and stay more or less manageable. Hopefully our young sons Ben and Alfie will inherit your best patterns!

Contents

Foreword by Joan Borysenko   xiii

PART ONE:
CHANGING YOURSELF

1. Fed Up with Trying to Change?   3

2. Where Are You Now?   21
Step One: Awareness   21

3. What Do You Really Want in Life?   35

4. Releasing Your Issues   49
Step Two: Expression   49

5. Healing Your Past   64
Step Three: Forgiveness   64

6. Making Peace and Moving Forward   78

7. Ending the Battle Between Your Emotions
and Your Thoughts   91

8. Living Life Fully Again   110
Step Four: New Behaviour   110

PART TWO:
CHANGING YOUR LIFE

9. Transforming Your Approach to Love   140

10. Enriching Your Relationships with
Friends and Colleagues   157

11. Choose Your Work. Don't Let it Choose You   179

12. Getting Beyond Compulsive Patterns   202

13. Spirits in a Material World   222

14. Tune into Your Body   234

15. Celebrating Your Sexuality   250

16. The Courage to Change   260

Appendices   268

Foreword

There are moments in every lifetime when the tide turns and you are forever changed. Long after such moments pass, you can recall them with an almost crystalline clarity. They seem realer than real, imbued with a singular richness of insight, emotion and Presence. In that instant you step out of the trance of daily life into a state of awakening and freedom. You are at home at last, comfortable in your own skin, feeling what Einstein called solidarity with all life. Your personal journey – the successes and failures, the wounds and the wisdom – makes profound sense. A wellspring of compassion opens, and you love yourself and all beings with deep humility and utter simplicity – perhaps for the very first time. From that tender place of homecoming comes the absolute conviction that life is a sacred journey, a blessing and a privilege.

I experienced such a moment of awakening over a decade ago during the Hoffman Quadrinity Process. I had already done much of the work that you will do in the first section of this book, identifying the patterns of behaviour that had caused so much pain in my life. But the understanding was largely intellectual until our group played a simple game together. One person stood in the centre of the circle and made some kind of funny motion, like jumping around in a circle or flapping their arms. The rest of the group had to mirror their antics. The person in the centre then chose someone else from the circle to be 'it'. I was the last one chosen. It felt achingly like being back in grammar school again, viewing life from the sidelines.

As I stood in the circle watching my classmates I felt more and more self-conscious. I would gladly have disappeared from the face of the earth rather than stand there for one more minute. Since I was a psychologist, medical scientist and author used to giving frequent lectures to large crowds, as well as leading intimate personal growth workshops, you might wonder why I felt so uncomfortable. Everyone else seemed playful. They were having a ball. I stood there poised and smiling, self-contained and apparently confident. But it wasn't really any fun at all. In fact, I wanted to throw up.

My teacher in the Hoffman Process was Tim Laurence, the author of the book that you are holding in your hands. A few hours after the game, he called me aside. Why, he inquired with great respect and interest, did I think that I was the last one to be chosen? I froze. My breath stopped. I turned red. 'Damn it, caught out,' I thought.

I racked my mind for plausible excuses that might restore some dignity to my bruised ego. At the same time, I realised that there was nowhere to hide. I had signed up for the Process to face my behavioural patterns and to create a future different from my past. Honesty seemed the last best hope. It was clear that there was no way out but through.

'I am so self-contained that I scare people away, don't I?' I said in a small voice, a child's voice. 'I am a know-it-all. An Ice Queen.' My carefully wrought, polished, professional persona fell away and I began to sob, 'How can I play when I hate myself? Whatever I am is never enough. No one could love who I really am.' Now I was getting somewhere. My false self, or ego, had cracked and fallen away. Inside was a familiar pain and fear that I had carried around in secret for a lifetime. It cried out for healing.

Tim witnessed my emotional pain with absolute kindness. And he didn't let me off the hook. He asked questions that helped me stay with the feelings that I was experiencing. Whereas my intellect had talked a good game all my life, it hadn't changed how I felt. I was perpetually uptight and unable to play and be spontaneously present. Instead, all my energy went into projecting an image that I felt would look good to others. My emotional reactions were those of a small child, still looking for love and acceptance. I saw clearly how my body was caught in a constant crossfire between the rationalisations and postures of my intellectual self and the fear and sorrow of the small child inside. The warring voices of my intellectual and emotional selves created stress that had shown up as migraine headaches, muscle tension, stomach problems and other physical symptoms. In fact, it was those very illnesses that had gotten me interested in mind/body medicine two decades earlier.

But in spite of all the studies and sincere efforts to heal my life, I hadn't really changed. I had just become a more insightful neurotic. Finally, with Tim's help, I had come to a turning point. In that moment of awareness and honest emotional expression I was able to glimpse my own innocence and forgive myself. This proved to be a lasting foundation for new behaviours. It enabled me to do what the book offers you – to create a future different from my past.

Since that moment I have been a champion of the Hoffman Quadrinity Process, and currently serve as Chairman of its advisory board. Every month I get letters from grateful people who have found the Process through my writings and come to a new level of awareness and action through the beautifully designed programme that is now available to you not only as an eight-day residential programme, but through working with this book. As a psychologist, medical scientist and author of ten books on stress, healing, health and spiritual growth, I can attest to the elegance of this healing system.

If you have come to the point where you are fed up with being fed up, you are ready to change your life. What you have here is skilful means to begin your transformation. The programme in this book is the finest and most complete expression of what healing and spirituality are all about. If it was the only book available on psychospiritual transformation it would be enough. Tim has done a superb job describing the steps that you need to take, bringing many years of experience into these pages. All you need to bring is your sincere desire to create a better life for you, your family, the people that you work with and our troubled world. That is spirituality in action. And it is the truest expression of love. It is what you were born for.

Joan Borysenko, Ph.D.

PART ONE

CHANGING YOURSELF

1

Fed Up with Trying to Change?

*God regards with merciful eyes not what you are nor what
you have done, but what you wish to be.*

THE CLOUD OF UNKNOWING

Have you tried to change but, even with the best of intentions,
ended up doing the same old things in the same old ways?
You've read the books, gone on various courses and bought
the T-shirt, made firm resolutions and even told all your
friends about those promises, only to return swiftly to the same
old place in your life? Sometimes you even feel worse and then
you beat yourself up for breaking your own promises. You still
feel overweight, you're still dissatisfied in the same job, you
still follow the same old cycle of 'I love you and can't live
without you – I hate you and don't ever want to see you again'
in your relationships. Sound familiar?

Bob Hoffman was working in San Francisco, leading individual sessions, when it became clear that he was often hearing
the same old stories about people getting stuck. His clients
were usually the world-weary types who had tried just about
everything else, and had come to him through desperation.
He felt there had to be another way beyond merely talking
things through. What could enable someone to change

fundamentally? Over the course of several years, he came to develop his own practice of moving people through the blocks in their lives. He earned a very solid reputation among a circle of San Francisco area psychiatrists and therapists by helping some of their toughest clients. They had referred these people when more traditional methods failed.

From 1967 until his death in 1997, he worked first in the US, then in South America and continental Europe, and, finally, in the UK. The culmination of his techniques was 'The Hoffman Process', a sequence of exercises that moves us from *Awareness* of our blocks to finding *Expression* for them, followed by self-*Forgiveness* and, finally, *New Behaviour*.

BOB WHO?

When I first met Bob Hoffman, I had an interview with him that probably lasted not much more than half an hour. But during that short time, he managed to touch me deeply. I cried for the first time in months, suddenly aware of my sense of loneliness. I got angry at the injustice I had felt as a child. I laughed at his crazy wisdom. With his help I saw a higher reality, beyond my normal consciousness. *This is how I want to live*, I told myself as I left the interview. *I want to feel all parts of me fully alive again*.

Bob was part genius, part crazy fool. He was the wisest of men and the simplest. I never saw him reading a book on psychology, but he knew more about the human mind than most of my former teachers put together. He was deadly serious about helping people to leave their pain behind, and had a terrible sense of humour that delighted in appalling puns. He could melt you with his doleful eyes and find the right buttons to drive you madly angry. He could call you a sensitive, loving person and an hour later say you were being a two-faced phoney. He did not live by the normal rules and took great risks in – as he put it with characteristic lack of modesty – 'pushing people towards Heaven'. So if he discovered or just sensed that you were stuck in a pattern, he would march right in there, all five feet six of him, with his psychic surgeon's knife.

Bob Hoffman was not a qualified psychologist or psychiatrist. His knowledge of the human condition was one based on his intuition, as well as direct experience – of his own life and the lives of his clients. He was a formidable natural psychologist, a gift shared by many people who closely watch the cast of characters and their display of human nature around us. Perhaps it was his *lack* of formal education that enabled Bob to see through the layers of denial in his clients. When I first tried to blind him with my own knowledge – terrified of course that he might see the real me underneath – he looked at me kindly but directly in the eyes and said, 'You can't fool me. I'm too ignorant.'

Bob was a gifted psychic, and wanted to use his gift to help others. He realised that the brightest of people could fall into self-destructive behaviour, so the answer could not lie in intellectual reasoning. He saw that there was a gap in our comprehension of the world, a gap that no body of teaching had yet approached.

The gap, Bob realised, was that we learn our habits emotionally; therefore, we can only come to healing by releasing emotionally. This could not be done by talking. It had to be done by expressing the full range of emotions and then arriving at a complete sense of compassion for our parents and ourselves. It was to be a new education, a re-education of the emotional part of ourselves.

He tested out this theory, and it worked – so much so that the professional community started beating a path to his door. He was persuaded to train a group of therapists in his method. Now Bob was never really one to write things down.

Fortunately for him, he found willing helpers to make a method of what came to him naturally. He named his theory the Negative Love Syndrome, and the four-part model of our being, the 'Quadrinity'.[1]

THE PROCESS:
THERAPY, EDUCATION AND RITUAL

As a method of change, the techniques you are going to be using work in a variety of ways. They provide a bridge that few others have ever been able to build, or even imagined building. It's a bridge that connects therapeutic methods, not only to ones that appear to belong to the world of 'education' but also to methods and practices that belong to 'ritual'.

As therapy, the Process helps to identify and resolve issues of the past that affect our present lives, whether they involve relationships, work or career, or our roles as parents or as spiritual beings. It is not, however, concerned with making a diagnosis and listing personality disorders. Bob used to say, 'These are your patterns of behaviour', but quickly would add, 'but they are only patterns – you yourself are much more.' Instead, the Process aims to build up a healthy sense of self that does not need to rely on others, especially parental and authority figures, but that can stand independent and willing to take responsibility for its own actions. A healthy ego is one that is centred in itself first, and has worked on its own development through the various stages, from the healthy 'no' of a two-year-old, through the rebellion of a teenager, to leaving home both literally and metaphorically when we come of age.

[1] For more on the origins and developments of the residential Hoffman Process, please refer to Appendix B (see page 271).

As 'education', the Process teaches that we can be led out (the Latin *e-ducare* means exactly that) from old patterns of behaviour and can be taught – or, more importantly, teach ourselves – new ways of being. It is a very emotional education, meaning that we feel our way through it, and that way it lodges deeper within our own learning system. Without it, we would always have to have someone either doing the fishing for us, or being paid to teach us how to fish. This way we can go out and find food for our own nourishment.

As 'ritual', the Process makes real this passage into the world of self-responsibility. You may be already familiar with the work of Joseph Campbell, who spent his entire life enquiring into the universal rituals of the Hero's Journey. The stages he identified were:

* Separation – we leave our everyday world
* Initiation – we go through a series of tests
* Return – we take our learnings back into every day life

So it is with the Hoffman Process. Doing this work, you are taking time out of your regular life to undergo a set of tasks and challenges, a kind of inner search for the dragon. You confront this dragon, slay it (or sit down and have a cup of tea with it, learning the gift it can offer us) and then go back into your regular life again to apply what you have learned. You are forever 'marked' by this ritual.

THE HUMAN CONDITION:
FOUR ASPECTS MAKE US WHOLE

The three pillars of therapy, education and ritual build firm foundations upon which we can turn from a human *doing* into a human *being*. The Quadrinity Model plays a key role. Bob

Hoffman explained that we are composed of four parts, which he labelled the Quadrinity. These four parts are:

- our Emotions or feelings
- our Intellect or thoughts
- our Spirit or essence
- our Physical realm or body

All four parts will be involved as you work through this book.

Our Emotional self develops from birth onwards. Its function is to provide us with the feelings and emotions needed in order to develop enjoyable and productive relationships with others as well as ourselves. We need relationships to belong, to love and to be loved. When we experience any form of emotional deprivation as children, we acquire feelings of rejection, humiliation, abandonment and betrayal, which we recreate in our subsequent relationships. Our emotional well-being and growth can be stunted, and we do not mature emotionally. And childish patterns can remain. We say 'no' without thinking or automatically reply 'I can't do that' when facing a new challenge. We are petrified of standing up and speaking in public. 'What if I get criticised?' says the Emotional self childishly.

The Intellectual self develops from around six years onwards. Its function is to provide us with clear thought and reason, in order to make decisions in a healthy and rational way. It is required for the development of reason and to ensure survival as we continue to grow and mature. We are driven forward in the world by our need to know. When this is not encouraged or is over-stressed in childhood we develop feelings of being stupid, inadequate, confused or even mentally unbalanced.

A positive intellectual aspect provides us with good judgement and discernment. A negative aspect internalises the voice of the critical parent by saying 'Don't do that' and 'Don't be so stupid'. It has over-developed its critical faculty and turned it in on itself or always looks for faults in others. It's a side of us that is defensive, self-righteous, and hates to be wrong. Oh, and it loves to have the last word!

As emotional adults we would like to be able to respond and articulate our own feelings, but, sadly, many of us stay repressed or depressed. The worst part of it is that we don't even keep the childlike part of ourselves alive – the happy, enthusiastic spontaneous person inside. What we have in charge most of the time is a highly rational side, what Hoffman calls the 'Adult Intellect'. We believe that we have to look together, sound intelligent, be efficient and productive, and generally miss out on the fun. Indeed, fun and play are scorned by our Adult Intellect as being beneath consideration. This has disastrous consequences on our internal peace. At other times, it's the Emotional self or 'child' inside that is in charge, hijacking our responses to a situation. We come across as being dramatic and highly anxious, or we want to throw it all in.

A large emphasis of this Process is on reconciling the emotional (child or old brain) and intellectual (adult or new brain) aspects of your personality. Through this you can then integrate the four parts of your being. To enable this to happen, you first have the opportunity to explore in depth the relationship with your carers when you were children, and to understand the effect that these relationships have had upon your subsequent emotional, mental, physical and spiritual development.

By first understanding childhood experiences and then working through them, you will be able to separate yourself from rigid belief systems and parental character traits, as well as potential emotional trauma which may have been sabotaging your adult life in one way or another. Once this separation has occurred, you can experience a profound inner healing with long-lasting results.

> *You will be able to heal by letting go of the past.*
> *You will be able to live in the present.*

You will also be getting to know a part of you that is free from any programmes or conditioning. We call this part the Spiritual self, or essence inside. Think of it as the diamond that lives within each of us, the clear channel of light. It is always there, even if we are completely caught up in our own day-to-day struggles, the trivia of modern existence. It's the voice within, the part that leads us towards our greater potential. It is our connection with God and the Universe.

Your Spiritual self will be much more available to you once you look at and do some major house-cleaning on your own patterns. The Hoffman Process digs out the layers of encrusted mud that have accumulated over the years and lets you reconnect with your diamond essence. By doing this, you are led back to your own truth and your own vision of how things really can be. You are put back in touch with your own wisdom and intuition. You will learn to trust that the answers lie within. Your Spiritual self lets you experience love and joy, arising from a source that knows no limit.

The fourth element is one that you can touch and feel at any time. It's your physical reality, the body. Throughout this book, stay in touch with how your body responds when you feel an emotion. Stay in touch with your body when you go through a guided visualisation. Listen to its response under stress and in times of peace. Learn to honour its own magic and mystery. It's the home of your spiritual self during your lifetime. Don't become, as so many of us have, like the character in James Joyce's *Ulysses*, who 'lived a short distance from his body'!

How Can the Process help to change my life?

When you experience your wisdom and the power of things as they are, together, as one, then you have access to tremendous vision and power in the world. You find that you are inherently connected to your own being. That is discovering magic.

CHOGYAM TRUNGPA RIMPOCHE

The residential Hoffman Process has helped to change many lives, whether the human being inside is an astronaut or businessman, young student or retired fisherman, homemaker or teacher. It is a deep cleansing experience that allows each person to completely reassess everything about themselves and their belief systems in a safe and supportive environment. Sonia Choquette, author of *Your Heart's Desire*, said of her experience, 'In the Hoffman Process I experienced all aspects of myself cooperating instead of negotiating with one another, which I loved.'

How and why the Process is so effective is a hard question to answer, not least because it is very difficult in research to isolate all other factors and name those that contribute to change. However, over the years we have amassed a great deal of anecdotal evidence.

The first reason that people suggest is that they finally allow themselves to see the bigger picture, an image of themselves and the world that is not just coloured by the beliefs that they had held up to that point. They go beyond the patterns of their parents and the dominant culture to feel underneath what is true to them. They may also have a profound spiritual experience once the chatter of the mind has been emptied out, and shift their fundamental life values or goals as a result. For others, going through the dark periods of their lives can release a great deal of blocked energy, especially the energy they have needed to hold in fear, anger or sadness. That energy, now released, can be used for a positive direction; for example, in work or in relationships, and pay its own dividends in 'the real world'. Joan Borysenko also said that since doing the Hoffman Process herself, 'one of the most concrete changes I have experienced . . . is the steady increase of joy and gratitude that began to bubble up. Another change is that I find it nearly impossible to blame and shame myself or anyone else.'

At some point in our lives, we all feel the need to move on, to travel beyond what we already know. We experience a calling to learn and experience more than we have already learned or been taught. For some of us, that means travelling and exploring other cultures. For others, it means stopping work and training for another career.

All of us, however, can benefit by looking at what we learned, and probably take for granted, in the way we grew up. Even if we get on with our parents or carers very well, there are probably areas of our behaviour and reactions of which we are unaware. To us, these ways of acting or being are totally natural. But they might just drive other people up the wall! For instance, we expect to have a Sunday lunch with the rest of the family. Our partner, unused to such strong family bonds, wants to spend a quiet day without visitors. We are quite happy doing an undemanding job. How come everyone else sees this as being lazy and unambitious? We lavish gifts on our children. We get accused of spoiling them. We wonder whose way is the 'right' way.

Whatever our age, we need to leave the family nest properly, and to discover our own values. On a deep level, we carry around not only their sets of beliefs, but also their attitudes and even their feelings. Through the Hoffman Process, the beliefs and attitudes that limit us and are not authentically ours can be identified and changed. It is important to consider both the positive and negative way we view our parents and carers, because our lives may just be run by them. Resolving on a deep emotional level any old issues with our parents and carers, *even if we feel that intellectually everything is just fine with them* can very much alter the way we behave in the world, particularly to our loved ones and to those in authority positions, such as our bosses.

My personal story

As a curious child looking at my own life and those around me, I asked, from a very early age: 'Is that it? Surely there must be something more to life?'

Despite many years of travelling in order to look for an answer, nothing seemed to make me feel any better. I had studied methods of Western Psychology until I could bore anyone with so-and-so's theory of Cognitive Dissonance versus Determinism versus Behaviouralism. I had studied Eastern religions and meditated until I found that 'sitting quietly, doing nothing' did not result in a quiet mind. In fact, it gave me a live and distressing feed into my own brain with no chance of pleasant distractions. I had tried dancing, singing, aura reading, anger management, assertiveness training, T'ai Chi, Energy Balancing, Zen meditation and, of course, read hundreds of books. But . . .

Something, a big piece of the puzzle seemed still to be missing. Somehow I came to believe I had outsmarted all these methods designed to procure that elusive self-fulfilment. A curious child had grown into a cynical adult. I realised I was somehow only 'coping' with life rather than truly living it. The juice was running out of a relationship, work was feeling just more of the same, and I was muddling along with a constant low-grade depression. The question still haunted me – 'Surely there is something more to this? Do I grow up just to earn a living, buy a house and car, do my duty and then have a nice funeral?' All this, even though I was living in a log cabin on a beautiful wooded hillside in California.

When I was feeling particularly low, friends of mine started talking about a method called the Hoffman Process. I felt I wouldn't have the enthusiasm for yet another course – I was burned out and a lot lighter in the wallet than when I had begun my inner journey some ten years earlier. However, I became intrigued when they talked about its effect on them: 'Like an emotional roller-coaster'; 'a spring cleaning for the garbage inside'. I became hooked on the idea when Marian, a wise old soul from Brooklyn, told me, 'I never knew how much I was like my mother and father until I did the Hoffman Process.' Could I be like that, too? NO, no, no, no . . . yes! I was! Despite my intelligent rebellion, my self-image as the rebel with a profound cause, parts of me were very like my parents. Marian and I talked long into the night about family 'patterns', the behaviours and beliefs that are passed on from one generation to another, and how those patterns lived on in us. In my case, I could see that my emotional shut-down, my denial and my depression had all been inherited from the family environment in which I had grown up. Distrust of relationships could have begun when I was very young and saw my parents going through a divorce. I wondered, deep down, what was the point of staying with anyone?

I knew what the problem was. I just didn't know what to do about it. So I signed up in the hope that these patterns could be neatly removed. The Process was to be a week-long residential course in the sun-baked hills an hour east of San Francisco. Meeting Bob Hoffman on the first morning, I knew I was in the presence of someone quite extraordinary. I walked into the library of the conference centre and his laser eyes pierced into mine, letting me know without any doubt that there was no point in putting up my usual masks. He managed to convey this with compassion, which was a change from the full-on encounter style I knew only too well. Of all the teachers I have had, I consider Bob Hoffman to be the most brilliant educator of our own human potential. He was also possibly the most unorthodox, and was always ready to throw out the rule book if it slowed down his intuitive style.

By the time I met him, Bob was in his late sixties and had just returned from travelling the world for almost a year and a half. I would have expected him to be slowing down, but he seemed to have more energy than the other, far younger teachers on the course. He was everywhere at once. Being a gifted psychic, he could pick up on themes very quickly.

I had never seen myself as being a complaining type of person, so I was taken aback when Bob passed me in the corridor once and casually asked me if I had looked at my pattern of complaining.

'No,' I replied flatly. 'That's one pattern I don't have.'

'OK, so you've never ever complained about the service in a restaurant, never complained how much something cost?'

'Well, yes of course, but that isn't complaining, that's questioning.'

He smiled and moved on down the corridor. Turning around, he added, 'You might find it useful to look at whether you're defensive as well.'

Me defensive? Never! Except when I'm being challenged, criticised, given feedback, feeling guilty, asked a question, and so on . . . oh, no, back to work on myself.

My own journey in the Process started as a guided tour into the depth of my beliefs and attitudes, and ended as an uplifting voyage into the visions and realities of a higher consciousness. The Hoffman Process as a rite of passage had me take a walk back into childhood in order to be able finally to emerge into the world of adults. Like the real Hero's Journey, it marked me. I was different before it began and when it had finished, my friends all remarked on the change. Some of those changes were subtle, such as a greater calmness and more balanced moods. Some were obvious, like a leap in self-confidence that allowed me to start talking in front of groups of people. Or a belief that relationships could actually last so that I found my life partner and married her (what? me marry?).

When the course was nearly over, we had a session during which everyone got to share the reactions they had felt towards each other. When it was my turn to be on the receiving end, I could not see but felt that Bob had come around from the front to sit just behind me. More than half the group had had negative reactions to me during the week and he was there to listen and perhaps just check that I was not getting too defensive.

He met me after that session and said, 'I may have a job for you.'

I thought he meant doing some translations so that his work could be understood in other countries.

'No,' he said, 'I want you to think about becoming a teacher of this work.'

'Thanks,' I said.

'Don't thank me, someone has already decided,' he retorted.

That, of course, got me thinking. The next day something must have been written on my face, because Bob came up and said, 'Don't worry if you can do it or not. I've checked you out.'

I imagined that he had his office put in a call to the

FBI to see if I had a criminal record. It was only years later, when I knew him much better, that I found out what he really meant.

'I asked my friends up above. They always have the right answer,' he replied, referring to his spirit guides that, as a psychic healer, he often consulted.

I had a dream that last night of the course. I was in a field full of huge electric pylons. I was climbing up one pylon to connect a power line from it to another pylon. Bob was below me on the ground, shouting up, 'You can do it.'

In my dreams or awake, Bob was right, for I took to the training like a duck to water. Because I'd studied psychology I found the premises easy to understand, without being too bogged down in the thick mire of theory. I loved working with a team of people rather than doing sessions alone, where I or the client might become discouraged with the slow pace of progress. The performer in me thoroughly enjoyed being 'front of room' to give a presentation. And the part of my character that loves to act, thrilled to the drama of the Process. It's like a tragi-comedy with a rich cast of characters that constantly changes. Though I had worked at both the Berkeley Holistic Health Center and taught at the University of California, Berkeley, I was ready to give up my past life and throw myself into this work that so skilfully weaved together elements from Gestalt, Family Systems Theory, Psychodynamics and Bioenergetics. On top of it all, it was a process that trusted in the essential health and good-ness of humanity. It neatly spanned the gap between an analysis of our past, favoured by the traditional psychotherapies but also the credo of the Humanistic Movement that states that it is not so much where we come from, but what we can do that matters.

I have now taught this Process to thousands of people from many different cultures, in half a dozen countries and a handful of languages. Many years on it continues to inspire me and that inspiration carries forth in my passion to continue this work. I started by working in the United States and then also in Canada, where they needed someone to oversee their new centre and teacher-training programme. Later I faced another challenge, of delivering the course in French, albeit as a member of an international team.

Perhaps, however, the biggest challenge was in returning to teach it in the country of my upbringing, England, which was also the last time I worked with Bob leading a Process. Being one who loves to take on new challenges, I then decided that moving back to England would be interesting, to put into practice the newly healed relationship with my past, and to rediscover what it was like seeing the land with new eyes that could respond rather than just react. As a seasoned traveller, I was testing Proust's maxim: 'The real challenge lies not in seeking new landscapes, but in seeing them with new eyes.'

I have done this work of connecting powerful energies for more than twelve years now. It has challenged me and rewarded me far more than anything I had ever done before that. It is my true Life's Work.

HOW THIS BOOK CAN CHANGE *YOUR* LIFE

This book sets out the richness of those teachings that have changed not just my own life, but many lives around the world. It explains the theories and methods that power the residential Hoffman Process, and describes the very practical tools that can be used in daily life to ensure those changes last. It is there for you to use, enjoy, share and pass on to others.

I encourage you to participate fully in the exercises throughout this book. If you allow yourself to go along with their movement, you will be swept along as if on the crest of a wave that has immense power to move and change you. Follow the cycle of the four most important steps: Awareness, Expression, Forgiveness, and New Behaviour, and you will find yourself moving on from old issues that have kept you in a rut. You really *can* change your life.

Awareness sets us out on the journey of exploration. It's an awareness that must come with a ruthless honesty. We can be aware of our own self-destructive behaviour and then interpret it to suit ourselves, saying 'It's not such a big deal' or 'I really don't care'. It's an awareness that has to be objective. Either we have the discipline to be objective with ourselves or we get the people close to us to tell us how they see us. The main question we ask at this stage is: 'What are the patterns of behaviour that get in the way of who I really am?'

Expression is the next step. To let go of our behaviour patterns, we need to let out the excess energy holding them in. We might write it out, or yell in the shower, or run with it, jogging it out of our systems and into the pavement. We can dance, stomp, even laugh it out. The important part is not to let the energy, which is usually an old, blocked emotion, stay and drag us down. The question at this stage is, 'What do I need to do to lessen the charge of this pattern?'

The third step is Forgiveness. We may have made mistakes, and we know that others have made them as well. To take charge of our own lives, we need to forgive ourselves for the mistakes of the past, and to forgive others for their mistakes. If we have been hurt or hurt others, we need to take a radical look at letting go and forgiving so that we can wipe the slate clean and move on.

Finally, and providing the proof of change, is New Behaviour. What new practices can we put into effect? The learning becomes effective in the doing. All along, we will see that there are new, positive ways of behaving to replace the old ways that have worked against us for so long.

The first part of this book outlines the underlying structure of the Hoffman Process. You begin by looking at the patterns that run your life and work on the ones that you most want to change. You learn to let go of the influence of the past. Next you go on to resolve any conflicts between your rational and your emotional sides, freeing you from compulsive behaviour and putting your life in balance. Your spiritual side can then guide you on the path of wisdom and truth. By the end of the first part, you will have taken charge of your life and discovered new ways of acting and being. The second part of the book then applies the essential tools of the process to the various areas of your life, especially love and work. By using these tools you can not only work through unresolved issues, but you can also keep yourself clear and focused in the present.

The Hoffman Process is a powerful catalyst for changing your life. Even though you are not experiencing the full impact of the residential course, by using this book you can take huge steps in your own self-development. Walk on this path wisely and you will be rewarded many times over. May you make it your own interesting and healing journey and have the courage to throw yourself into it fully.

2

Where Are You Now?

Step One: Awareness

The unexamined life is not worth living.
SOCRATES

To make even one change in our lives, we have to be very honest about how things *really* are. We have to take a good look at our current state of affairs. How we feel about our lives will motivate us to change. But this kind of honesty comes with a warning: It could seriously affect your lifestyle.

ASSESSING YOURSELF

Make a self-assessment from 0 to 10 in the areas described below. 0 is very bad and 10 is excellent. Be honest!

How would you assess your:

☐ Opinion of yourself
☐ Ability to perceive your own feelings
☐ Ability to convey your feelings to others
☐ Ability to approach others
☐ Ability to change undesired patterns of behaviour
☐ Trust in the future
☐ Understanding of the spiritual part of your being
☐ Ability to enjoy life
☐ Ability to spend time on your own

How would you assess your relationship with:

☐ Your mother
☐ Your father
☐ Your surrogate mother (e.g. stepmother or grandmother)
☐ Your surrogate father (e.g. stepfather or grandfather)
☐ Your children
☐ Your brothers and sisters
☐ Your spouse/partner
☐ Your friends
☐ Your colleagues at work/college

Where are the highs and lows? Are there areas that you really want to look at, and others that you feel are already well handled? Is there an imbalance between the comfort of spending time alone (10) versus the ability to approach others (0)? What is your first reaction to your score?

The first and most important question is how you feel about yourself. Your responses to the other questions depend on your answer to this one. For if you don't feel that great about yourself, it's going to affect your feelings, your trust, your time alone and, of course, all of your relationships, with family, friends and work colleagues.

HOW'S YOUR LOVE LIFE?

One of Bob Hoffman's favourite questions – even or especially if it bugged people – was 'How's your love life?' What he meant by this was not if we were in love or getting enough sex, but whether we loved *ourselves* first. His definition of love was: the flow, the outpouring of emotional goodness to yourself first, and then to others around you.

Selfish? It certainly sounds that way, but then consider the safety demonstration that takes place before every plane flight. We are told that if the oxygen masks drop, mothers should put them on their own mouths before covering their babies'. It seems counter to instinct, but of course it makes sense. The mother is no good if she's passed out from oxygen deprivation. We are no good if we are not able to feel any love for ourselves.

If we are love-deprived, we are going to act out. It may be that we overwork and forget when we need to rest. This can lead to resentment, burn-out and chronic fatigue syndrome. It may be that our attitude to food is unhealthy, and we use it to literally fill up the emptiness we feel inside, leading us into a never-ending cycle of bingeing and dieting. For some, watching TV fills the void. 'Reality TV' or the soaps or the sitcoms provide endless hours of looking at other people's lives rather than our own. Why would we want to, if we suspect all is not well there?

Without self-love, we also may find it more tempting to seek out the company of others and avoid simply being with ourselves. Many so-called friendships are founded on taking care of one another. The unspoken contract might be, 'I'll make you feel slightly better if you help remove some of my misery.'

In relationships with our husbands, wives or partners, it could get even messier. You got together when you were in love, and now the first bloom of romance is over, it's a day-to-day power struggle. You might even contemplate leaving each other, except that you'd feel even worse alone.

If you find it hard even to be in a relationship, how much of that is because you find it hard to put up with yourself? If you find it hard to relax in your own company, what's it going to be like for your date? When you make negative remarks about yourself to your lover, you are giving them two tough choices. They either believe it, which is going to send you further into despair, or they have to rebut it. But if you don't believe you're beautiful, talented and gorgeous, it's going to take a lot of effort on their part, and eventually they'll tire and become resentful of making that effort.

Neurosis is nothing more than the state of feeling unlovable. If you could choose just one thing to change, how about being able to feel, 'Just as I am, I am loveable.' It is this inner shift the Process aims to accomplish on a deep emotional level.

The first step, then, is Awareness.

What do you feel are the major problems in your life right now? Do you feel stuck somewhere, whether in a relationship or career, or that you have no access to certain feelings? Do you experience low self-esteem or feel depressed much of the time? Do you yearn for a deeper spiritual connection, and find it hard to just *be*? Or is it everything? You would like to trade your life in and get another one, preferably with a larger bank account. Make a mental note of what you feel are your main issues, or write them down so that they become clearer in your mind.

You are learning to confront yourself. Remember that the original meaning of 'confront' is to bring things face to face. This is what you are doing. You are bringing your own issues right in front of your face – with the purpose of establishing the truth.

How do you feel about how you act in life? Are there behaviours over which you feel you have no control? You get angry at little things. You become uncontrollably sad at times and feel full of despair. You have this self-destructive streak that manages, just as you are on the brink of attaining success, to 'snatch defeat from the jaws of victory'. Perhaps on the other hand you are a perfectionist, so that nothing is ever good enough and you never feel satisfied. Do you have any substances or activities over which you also feel no control? Food, drink, even *having* to shop or clean or worry compulsively?

Inviting feedback from others

To further up the ante, if you are willing to take the risk, invite other people in your life into an 'awareness circle'. This will be a group of trusted people who together form a loving round-table of honesty. These people do not want to criticise you, but are willing to help you see even more about yourself. Perhaps they have also worked on their issues and are aware of steps they need to take in their own development. Take time over the next few days to talk to people like this who you feel close to – your partner, friends and even children, if they are old enough. Ask them to tell you honestly, and lovingly, what they see in you that could be called a negative behaviour. If it feels safer to you, invite someone skilled in communication to facilitate a meeting between you and the others.

Try just to listen without becoming involved in a discussion about it, and don't put them off by becoming defensive: 'I'm impatient? What about you? Look at how cross you were when I was only five minutes late yesterday!' This exercise may not be easy for you, but it is a marvellous opportunity to start taking down some walls. You may be surprised at the effect it has on opening up some of your relationships. Approach it with the intention of wanting greater awareness and honesty in your life.

PATTERNS THAT RUN OUR LIVES

Behaviours that recur again and again are known as 'patterns'. Just as with dominant themes that run through the design of a carpet or fabric, you can find dominant patterns that run through your life. They may even be so apparent that they are all you and your circle of friends and acquaintances can recognise in you. The patterns have become you.

Let's consider some possible patterns that may be running your life. From the list below, choose the patterns that *most* fit you. Be honest with yourself. They do not have to be ones that you do *all* the time, but they have a strong hold on you.

perfectionist	quitter
blamer	workaholic
victim	manipulator
know-it-all	seducer
pessimist	bossy
goody-goody	arrogant
control freak	self-righteous
pleaser	feeling guilty
worrier	fear of success
withholder	

When you have done that, take time to contemplate the effect of those patterns on your life. When and where do they really kick in? At work or at home? With your lover, with your colleagues, or just with you? You may notice that they have a harmful effect. They arrive as that nagging voice inside your own head that won't let you relax. You become critical of yourself or others and no longer can enjoy yourself. Think of specific situations in your life recently when you have lost your sense of peace or given away your power. If there's been an emotional reaction, there's probably been a pattern acting underneath.

One way to catch a pattern, therefore, is to identify when you feel out of sorts. You get more impatient or frustrated, flustered or upset. You 'lose it' when the 'it' is your normal sense of self. If you can identify and name the pattern, then you are able to see the 'brick in your own wall'. You are no longer blind to the reality. Confronting yourself may not make you feel any better yet, but it's a step you simply have to take to start making changes in your life. If you see it, you can do something about it.

Patterns that run specific areas of our lives

The problem is that patterns or traits become so ingrained in our unconscious that they begin subtly to run the different areas of our lives. The result? We actually *become* them. They have control over us, rather than *us* having control over *them*. We forget that we might still have a choice.

A pattern is:
a reaction that is negative
. . . compulsive
. . . automatic
. . . emotionally charged
and
. . . *learned!*

This last part is the good news because you can unlearn it. In doing that, you can once again exercise your own free will of how to *respond* to a situation rather than *react* to one.

PATTERNS IN EVERYDAY LIFE

Ready to go to work? Consider how patterns appear in different areas of your life. That way, you see the different bricks rather than one solid wall around you. Remember, this is an exercise to achieve a clearer insight into your life. It's not a mechanism to provide greater criticism of who you are! Patterns are what you *do*, not who you *are*.

Love Patterns:
fear of intimacy
neediness
withdrawn
dependent
abandoning

Sex Patterns:
believe sex is bad/dirty
fear of performance
cold/shut down
don't deserve pleasure
sexually provocative/
  seductive

Work Patterns:
workaholic
feel trapped
has to be boss
fear of success
fear of failure

Image Patterns:
'appearance is everything'
needs to be special
self-obsessed
status conscious

Money Patterns:
fear of poverty
has to spend to feel OK
manipulates through
  money
'money is everything'
'money is the root of all
  evil'

Power Patterns:
has to have own way
manipulative
intimidating
submissive
plays victim

Responsibility Patterns:
indecisive
no goals
avoids commitment
acts helpless

Invalidation Patterns:
perfectionist
critical
nit-picker

Next, look at how patterns can dominate your emotional state.

Fear Patterns:
fear the worst
fear of being abandoned
fear of engulfment
fear of change
fear of confrontation

Anger Patterns:
loses temper easily
revengeful
argumentative
sarcastic
lashes out – physically or
        verbally

How was that for you? Were you able to 'own' some of them, without feeling worse about yourself? Did you manage to take responsibility for them without beating yourself up? (If you are giving yourself a hard time about them, that's another pattern!) Now that you're more aware, what do you do with this extra knowledge? This is where most of us get stuck and then try to make it liveable. As one dear student of mine put it, 'I dug myself a rut, and then comfortably furnished it.' If we are comfortable, why would we want to look for a way out? What we need to do is to understand how these patterns are harming us or the people around us.

TASK FOR THE DAY

What things about yourself would you most like to change? Is it your impatience, your procrastination or your inability to finish a task? Is it that you have lost faith in yourself or in your partner? Is that you do not feel able to experience many emotions, or that you are a workaholic?

Look back on the list of patterns above and on page 26 if you need some ideas.

- Be aware of these patterns in your life. Do you feel that they take you over, leaving you no choice to respond to a situation? Spend a day with them, simply observing their effect. Do this until you have convinced yourself that they are worth dumping! Repeat this on another day with some other patterns if you want even more clarity about the difficulties in your life.

- Keep those feelings of frustration inside of you for now. Yes, sit on them today! It's when you realise that you are frustrated that you get the driving force for the next step towards change, which is expression. Then, when you let the frustration go, the release of the patterns is much more powerful. As an added benefit, your emotions, intellect and body will all really remember the release and reinforce that change.

When patterns become our roles in life

Is this who I really am?

When patterns take over our lives, all aspects of our being are affected. In terms of the Quadrinity, our spiritual selves are no longer our guiding voice. We are run instead by our emotional and intellectual selves, which have taken on all these patterns. We begin to find it more 'natural' to walk around operating behind a mask of patterns. We grow up and that mask of patterns becomes so entrenched that we forget we have what lies underneath – an essence or spiritual self. We adopt roles to cope with the world. We even come to believe that our roles in life are who we really are.

When one pattern takes over a large part of your life, it becomes your main role. Can you see this yourself? Think of the main role you play out in life. Do you get labelled, for example, the oversensitive one, the authoritarian, the problem, the wild one, the charmer, the boss, the drunk? Do you get trusted with all the difficult jobs – the strong one, perhaps? Or does everyone beat a path to your door when they have problems: you get to play therapist. The point is that it's worth seeing and dealing with if it's getting in the way of who you really are.

Who do you ask if you are not sure of what role you play in life? Just as you did in the feedback exercise to expand your 'awareness circle' (see page 25), set yourself a new challenge and ask the people close to you in your life, and then your work colleagues. You may even have two leading roles, one at home and the other at work; for example, complainer and motivator.

Here are some of the perennial favourites. Which ones most fit you?

princess	slob
rebel	fighter
clown	perfect one
black sheep	the damaged
special one	the sensitive
genius	troublemaker

peacemaker	complainer
star	misfit
baby	success
hero	failure
victim	angry one
sufferer	rescuer
dreamer	wild one
loser	disappointment
scapegoat	teacher
burden	spoilt one
sick one	invisible one
needy	goody goody

As a way of loosening their grip on you, think of where you might have started playing these roles. You may have evolved and become more subtle over the years, but I bet you began way back when you were a child. First, think of your position in the birth order. If you were the eldest child, you may have been given the responsibility of taking care of others, and now this feels completely natural to you. You just expect to have to take care of other people and the details in their lives. Meanwhile, other people expect you to be responsible, which allows them to forget things and drives you crazy. If you were the youngest child, on the other hand, you may have always been looked after so that you never needed to take responsibility. Someone will always be there to pick up the pieces. The role of the youngest child is to be 'Special' or 'Princess', which is fine until they leave the family for the real world. Do you know anyone who acts like that all the time?

I learned to get attention by being clever. I could come home from school and show my mother or father my work with the teacher's comments on it, and receive their praise. Aha, I thought, this is how I can make them spend more time with me. I'll become the best in the school. And I did. I routinely got the highest grades and became teacher's pet. I don't recommend it as a way of being voted most popular among your peer group, though. In fact, I lost out on friends.

Being the clever one became my firm role throughout my school and university career. I then took this into my work life and immediately got frustrated. How come I have to take orders from others? How come they are so much slower on the uptake than I am? Again, I wasn't winning any popularity contests nor long-term employment contracts.

So patterns can become the roles we play again and again. They become automatic and compulsive and are very hard to break.

The romance of the rebel

Sometimes we believe we are being different, when actually we are just acting out patterns. Again, it's not a choice, but a reaction.

A great friend of mine called Janey grew up as the third of four children with a school principal as a father. She even attended his school. He was a stern disciplinarian and expected his children to obey all the rules. Janey's brothers and sisters did exactly that, which left her with an interesting choice. Her emotional self as a child started thinking, 'If I want more attention in this family, I won't get it by being good. So I'll act out and then I'll get to spend some time with Dad.' She became the black sheep of the family, routinely being invited into his study to spend some 'quality time' with him, which meant, of course, being told off.

When she grew up, Janey put her energy into writing. Her passion for life was unbounded by the normal constraints of society and she established a good reputation for wonderfully original screenplays. However there was a downside. Her internal radar was so attuned to rules, and she was so vigorously opposed to accepting them, that even helpful suggestions became orders from above. Producers and other writers simply could not work with her and she developed a reputation for being difficult. Being the black sheep was no longer serving her. Her work dried up. With no money coming in, she had a very practical motivation to change, and change she did. Bit by bit, she came to understand how she operated. She really worked on the subconscious pattern of rebellion and made a commitment to replace it with new, positive behaviour. She regained her reputation, but with a big difference. She was motivated by an internal creative spirit, not by wanting to break the rules and be different.

COMPLETING THE FIRST STEP OF THE PROCESS

If we live in a role or hard-set pattern all the time, it no longer helps us. Instead it becomes our prison. We have to get in touch with how fed up we are in order to drive our bid to break out of that prison.

The way out starts with having a good look at the reality we live in. By doing this, we identify the individual bricks in the walls around us. This 'Awareness without compromise' is a great catalyst, for it makes it impossible to continue to act blindly in the same old ways. So now that you have identified the roles you play and the patterns that run through your life, you have completed the first major step of the process. You may already be experiencing far greater clarity and resolve in your life.

Now you know what it is you have to fight *against*. You are ready to look at what you want to fight *for*.

3

What Do You Really Want in Life?

Imagination is more important than knowledge.

ALBERT EINSTEIN

You can use the tool of Awareness in many ways. In the last chapter we used Awareness to shed light on *what* we wanted to change in our lives. Another great use of Awareness is to consider *how* would we like our lives actually to be, and how we would like to be in them. Then we get even more motivated to go beyond the known and comfortable. We often know what we *don't* want in life, and long to be rid of what makes us miserable. Up to now, that's where most of our awareness has gone. The problem is, we are not so good at stopping long enough to sense what it is we might want instead.

To motivate change, we need to use on ourselves a very subtle variation of the old 'carrot and stick'. The stick we have already seen; it's the horror of going back into the patterns of frustration or self-defeat we know so well. The carrot is a vision of how our lives could be, not just without those old patterns, but with what we really want in them. To imagine that, we need to train our minds in a certain way to overcome the usual objections. Doing this, we create new pathways in our brain which release pleasant chemicals that create sensations to motivate us.

Do you have an idea of what life you would like to have if you were free of your old patterns of behaviour? Can you use your awareness to see the future?

Imagine just *one* thing you really want in life. It may be your perfect home, or a loving partner, or perhaps your dream job. How about winning an Oscar, getting a book published, or living in another country? Whatever it is, the moment you think of it, it inspires a clear vision in your mind and for a moment you become lost within that vision. It takes on an existence within your own consciousness.

Now direct your attention to how you are feeling as you imagine this vision. Perhaps your heartbeat is raised with the exciting prospect of creating this different reality. You feel determined to take the steps to make it come true. Let it rest deliciously in your mind for a while. Treat yourself – it's a natural feel-good chemical!

A couple of years into teaching this work, I decided to put to the test the visioning techniques I was encouraging others to use. After a busy travelling schedule, I had decided to spend some quiet time kayaking around some islands off Australia. Dragging my boat up a beach one warm afternoon, two young children rushed up, full of curiosity, and started playing with my various bits of gear.

I showed them how the paddle worked, and the rudder, and helped them into the boat. Their mother came up and we fell into a conversation about travelling and so on. I felt quite proud letting her know how independent and free-spirited I was. She then asked if I had any children of my own, and I felt suddenly, and for the first time, very empty when I replied that I hadn't. That night, alone in my tent under the stars, the question 'Why not?' tore at my heart. I found myself aching with the pain of missing out on something so beautiful. The next morning I finally admitted to myself how much I wanted a stable relationship and a family of my own. So I started thinking – what kind of woman did I want to draw into my life? I needed someone with a calm temperament to counterbalance my fiery tendencies. Someone with a love of the outdoors and a career of her own that funnelled her creativity. I even asked that she have her own house (I'm not very good on interiors).

The vision found a place in my mind and then I forgot it, at least consciously. But something must have been working for me. Two months later, in London, I was invited to a West End theatre where, lo and behold, the leading actress happened to be someone I had met fourteen years earlier, when she was still at school. She was very beautiful. It was uncanny how similar she was to the person I had envisioned. As soon as I saw her on stage, that old cliché happened to me – I heard wedding bells ringing. I couldn't take my eyes off her, and immediately after the performance, I went backstage to see her. We chatted and exchanged phone numbers . . . We have now been married for many years and have two gorgeous sons. So I can say, from my own personal experience, visioning really does work.

You are about to get to work on your own vision, with the exercise below. Before you start, however, do keep in mind the old adage: Be careful what you pray for. You just might get it!

SO WHAT IS IT THAT YOU WANT IN YOUR LIFE?

When was the last time you listed your dreams and your heart's desires? Give yourself the treat right now of imagining a wonderful future.

Take a pen and a piece of paper and write down some things – off the top of your head – that you would like to achieve. Don't think about it, just write quickly without self-censorship. We are not talking about material possessions – most of us in the developed world have far too many of those anyway – but about manifestations of inner values. They might be things like a great love relationship, a healthy body, an overseas adventure, success in a particular field . . .

With your mind engaged in this, let's now work through various areas.

Focus your attention on your life – the way you would really want it to be if you could have it any way you wanted it. Imagine that you're not just surviving or doing all right, but passionately loving your life. Make your vision as specific as possible and include all areas of your life and lifestyle. Although this is how you are imagining it, pretend it is there in this moment. Use the first person present tense, for example: 'I have a very nourishing relationship with my partner, spending most evenings with him/her. My health is excellent, and I enjoy exercising by going for a brisk walk every morning.'

First experience your relationship with yourself – how you feel about yourself and treat yourself. Imagine being totally comfortable with yourself. You feel that your body is beautiful, alive and energised. You are in radiant health.

You know how to rest and be quiet, and you know how to challenge yourself. You feel at ease with yourself, both in your own company and with others.

Next, move on to see your relationship with the most significant people in your life: with your lover, your children, with other family members, and with your friends. See how well you are able to share yourself with them, how easy it is to be with them authentically and honestly. You not only enjoy their company, you thrive on it, sharing many moments of tenderness as well as laughter and creativity.

Now move on to your working life. What is it that you would most like to be doing? Actually see yourself there. It may be very different from what you are now doing, but imagine it nevertheless. You are expressing your creativity every day, contributing something useful to the world around you. It's not just work, it's your vocation, your calling. When you are not working alone, see the people around you at your work place and the relationships you have with them. Do you include each other in the creative fun of work as fellow team members? See yourself well rewarded for your work, and note that you and others put a good value on it. What is the balance between the time you spend at work and the time you spend with yourself, family and friends?

See the home you would like to live in. Where is it? What is around it? Is it in the city, the country, a small town or village? Is it near the mountains or the sea? Does it have a view? On the inside, do you have a place for entertaining guests as well as places to rest and reflect? Imagine it decorated in the style you find most pleasing.

See yourself giving time to your own 'being-ness', your

spirituality as you understand that term. Perhaps that means time meditating or praying, perhaps it's time in nature, perhaps with a group of fellow beings coming together to worship or perform rituals. Imagine how you nurture your own relationship with your essential spiritual nature.

Finally, see one thing that you would really want to be remembered for in your life. What is the special achievement that you would like to do or create? See yourself sailing across the ocean, at the book signing of your novel, making a film, travelling to explore this beautiful earth, or heading up a project in your community.

In all these areas, what is it that your heart really wants? If your heart does not speak, you will not become committed to that vision. Step into that vision. Experience it as if it really is your life. From that perspective, check in with yourself and ask: 'Is this what I really want?'

If you are not used to asking for much, this might be difficult. Take the limits off and for once ask your heart to show you all that it wants. Don't listen to that voice that says, 'This is ridiculous. You'll never be able to get that.' When you have the vision for your life clear in your mind, then say softly out loud, 'This is what I choose.' Experience yourself committed with all your heart to your vision. This way, you energise your motivation throughout all aspects of your being.

If you are pressed for time, or there's a chance of being interrupted in the middle of the exercise above, here's a shortcut to seeing what your heart really wants. In this short exercise, thinking for too long is strongly discouraged! Let yourself be surprised by what comes up.

Finish off these sentences as quickly as possible:

- If I could, I would . . .
- If I could, I would . . .
- If I could, I would . . .
- If I could, I would . . .
- If I could, I would . . .

And then to ratchet up the stakes:

- Before I die, I will . . .
- Before I die, I will . . .
- Before I die, I will . . .
- Before I die, I will . . .
- Before I die, I will . . .

Did you find things that you really wanted to do, but had been putting off? Let them sit inside you for now as you store their images. They will add fuel to the fires that burn deep within you.

REALITY CHECK

It's time to assess where you are in relation to your dreams and visions. After all, if your goal was to summit Everest, you would need to check how fit you were, how much climbing experience you had and how much knowledge of the path to the summit you had acquired. It would also be really useful to know whether you were starting from Kathmandu or Kentucky!

So be honest with yourself and look realistically at where you are now in your life. Let it be a truthful evaluation, neither too rosy nor too dark. Get a clear image of how and where you are today.

Consider the same areas for your reality check as you had in your vision:

- Self: your relationship with yourself, including your health.
- Relationships: your relationships with the most significant other people in your life, including spouse or partner, family and friends.
- Home: how comfortable do you feel where you live?
- Work and finances: how satisfied are you?
- Spirituality: do you have a relationship with a sense of a reality higher than the human one?
- Special project: are you engaged in something that lends greater meaning to your life?

Hold these images of your current reality and then breathe in your vision of what you want for your life. Be aware of both at once. Allow the difference between them to be there. The tension created by this difference is a creative one and it can serve you in moving toward your vision. Look at that vision once more and again say softly out loud, 'This is what I choose.'

What holds us back from achieving our vision?

When doing this exercise, you may have noticed that various old characters dropped in for a chat. By this I mean the voices in your head. What were some of the things that they were saying to you?

- Don't be ridiculous, you'll never get any of that.
- What makes you think you deserve that anyway?
- That's only for rich people, and they're all messed up anyway.

- Look why even bother to try and get it when you'll just lose it all?

Those old voices might not be able to imagine a different life from the one you have had up to now. None of your friends has the type of thing you dream of doing, having and being. So why should you deserve a miracle? Your intellect finds all kinds of reasons to knock you back to what it sees as normal reality. Then, alongside the reasoned response, there's the emotional one which goes much further back in time. This voice says, 'I can't imagine it because I didn't see it as a child. Mum and Dad weren't successful, so how can I be?' Locked in the past, it serves up its memories. Your mother and father may have had a lousy relationship. There was no sense of intimacy between them, unless you call the odd argument a display of intimacy. So why should you be able to go one better? If you keep hearing, 'I can't change the way things are', then consider how far back that belief goes. Who taught you all about being able to change and move on in life? 'But I wasn't born to sing, paint, design or write.' Where did you get *that* belief from? Know that it's not intrinsic to you, nor genetic. It's what you saw or heard in the past. It's not the only reality available to you.

Change the way you see the world, and your reality will change.

Which is why Einstein said that imagination was greater than knowledge.

THE FUNDAMENTAL MOTIVATION TO CHANGE: SEEING OUR SPIRITUALITY

Remember that when working on themselves, many people only see what's wrong with them. They might even become expert at diagnosing their own neurotic behaviour, and forget that there could be anything more. The danger of becoming aware only of the negatives in us is that we become drained of energy. It's hard to become excited about change when we feel tired and depressed.

If only we could keep at the forefront of our minds what is obvious to children and those on a dedicated spiritual path – who we *are* is far more than how we *behave*. If we truly *know* that, then we possess the driving force to overcome the chatter of the mind as well as the limiting statements of those around us. We would always have the energy to continue on the path of positive change.

Consider the following saying: 'We are not human beings having a spiritual experience. We are spiritual beings having a human experience.'

What would it take for you not just to believe that but to *know* it and let it motivate you throughout the day?

Vision work can lead you back to knowing that you are just that, a spiritual being having a human experience. You can use your mind to realise that you are much more than the sum of your patterns and the roles you occupy in life. This process of change guides you back to your true underlying nature, your Spiritual self. Once back in touch with this powerful aspect of your being, you have a truly precious gift throughout the journey of this process. It's yours to cherish, because after all, it's a part of you.

The following exercise gives you a direct experience of yourself as a spiritual being. By knowing that this part is always there, you start making that fundamental change. You not only see, but start to *know* that you are a spiritual being.

SEEING YOUR SPIRITUAL SELF

Think of a beautiful place in nature. It does not have to be one that you have visited. Let your imagination work to give you a picture of natural beauty. Imagine yourself there, with the sun shining down. It's as if you can even feel yourself being warmed by that sunshine. There may be a slight breeze around you. You smell how wonderfully fresh the air is with its scent of flowers. You feel relaxed and totally at ease.

Now feel yourself walking around this place. Do you see trees, grass, flowers, rocks? Fill in the scene. You are your own film director here. Let it be full of detail and colour. You find yourself feeling even more at ease. This is your *sanctuary*. Some call it the garden of their soul.

In this sanctuary, imagine there's someone coming up towards you. Looking closely at the person, you see that it's *you*. Yes, let yourself imagine that you're looking your best, with a radiance about you reflected in your eyes. Your face is without any lines of worry, but expresses wisdom and compassion. You sense that there is a quiet power inside of you born of thousands of years of experience. There's also an infinite well of love deep within this soul. If you close your eyes now, you can go deeper into this image of yourself. Breathe it in.

What you've imagined is a counterpart of yourself, one that is set free from the normal personality. Remember that the word 'personality' comes from the Latin '*persona*', meaning 'mask'. We spend most of our lives with masks in front of our true selves. Let us imagine the aspect *beneath* those masks.

In the sanctuary of your own mind, start getting to

45

know this other aspect of yourself. This is the being who brings you to make wise choices, even if all other parts are kicking and screaming and raising their objections in the usual old way. Here you have the spiritual component of the four aspects of your Quadrinity, your Spiritual self.

Make sure that you see your own face, and that you can see it as truly beautiful. You are unique, and your appearance radiates your unique beauty. Sure, there may be a voice saying, 'I'm not a model or anything. Of course I'm not beautiful.' Ignore it and see yourself that way. Even your hair is looking great today!

Stay with this image for a few minutes. Get in touch with how you feel inside. Remember the image and the feeling.

Now – here's a stretch – imagine you've fallen in love with this person. Having fallen in love, obviously you want to spend more time with them, get to know them, talk about life, and so on. It's a lot easier to imagine falling in love with someone else, isn't it?

Set yourself a small task. Instead of calling up your old friends or partner, imagine you're calling up this aspect of yourself, the part inside. You don't get on the phone or in the car, you simply close your eyes and 'call up' this inner aspect in your mind's eye. Spend a few minutes every day with this new friend. Ask him or her how he would lead life. How would he or she spend the time? Who would she hang out with? Would he spend the evening watching TV or doing something more creative? Does this aspect need to keep reading about disasters in the newspapers? Would this aspect put up with a dead-end job or relationship?

Take some time each day to go on a 'date' with yourself. It could be a walk, enjoying a fine meal in a restaurant, even taking time to relax in front of a beautiful view. Before you go to sleep, your date could be to lie in a warm soothing bath. Enjoy the feeling that you have a wonderful companion with you all the time.

The Spiritual self is the *unconditioned* part of ourselves. It corresponds to what other traditions call the Spirit or Essence. It's always there, like the very air we breathe. Like the air, we sometimes take it for granted and forget it until we are gasping for nourishment. Imagine it so that you can 'see' for yourself just how much more you are than the sum of your programmed personality.

Keep this aspect of yourself in mind as you work through the book. The essence of you is there in the background while we travel into the darker and more painful areas. It reminds us that we are far more than our old patterns and can aspire to far greater things than our old neurotic lifestyle. It's a gift you can return to again and again during this process of change. Seeing yourself with this bigger sense of self will motivate you to keep going through any challenging times on your personal journey.

TASK FOR THE WEEK

Visit your Spiritual self in your sanctuary for five minutes every day. Pressed for time? Two minutes then. You'll soon want to spend more time with this wise, quiet soul anyway. Ask this voice within for a special message for the day. What guidance are you ready to hear?

In order truly to change your life you need to change how you *see* yourself on the inside. Then you have a base from which to change how you *feel* about yourself.

You are now aware of *what* it is that you want to change; the patterns and the roles that have taken over your life. You have also discovered a vision of your life worth creating in reality. This is what you want to change *for*, and provides you with the energy and the motivation to move ahead.

The next step on the process of change is to express the old frustrations and limitations that have been stuck inside you. They have up to now prevented you seizing life by the horns and finding out who you really are. When you express them, you shake them off. They lose their power to undermine you. These old messages and beliefs have told you that you don't deserve a better life, or a good relationship, or an interesting career. And they are not true! In the words of Marianne Williamson, which became so well-known through Nelson Mandela's Inauguration Speech:

Who are you to be brilliant, gorgeous, talented, fabulous? Rather, who are you not to be?

4

Releasing Your Issues

It's one thing to use a pattern, and it's another to be used by it.
BOB HOFFMAN

Step Two: Expression

To change how we feel about ourselves, we need to express what has been stored up inside. Awareness of what we want and what we don't want is simply not enough. We need to let out our truth, and express the issues that have frustrated us, limited us or kept us in conflict. We need to find our own voice and reclaim our power.

You may have wondered why there are so many people who look burdened down by life. It's as if they are carrying a heavy piece of luggage around with them. Their posture is stooped, they wear the same fixed expression every day and they appear drained of energy. We listen daily to people talking about backaches, headaches and a myriad of other physical complaints. We are not at ease, we are at *dis*-ease with the physical aspect of ourselves. The dis-ease is the result of all the years when we have kept locked up what we need to express.

The body expresses what the mind represses. Even if we manage to stay unaware of the true state of our life, our body, with its own wisdom, will one day let us know what is stuck. But, of course, we can choose to ignore these very clear signals, expecting that a combination of talking, along with an anti-depressant and antibiotics, the latest fad diet or a session at the shopping mall, will lift us back into our vital life energy again.

But what is it we need to express? What is dragging our life force down? What's more, where can it go? We don't even have something or someone to dump it on!

CLEARING RESENTMENT

Here's a great exercise you can use to start your own expression and get some energy moving. You simply write or say in quick succession lots of sentences beginning with 'I resent': *I resent that my wife left this morning without saying good-bye. I resent that the traffic was so slow. I resent that Mike didn't turn up for the meeting. I resent being given so much work. I resent the weather. I resent weeds on my lawn. I resent that my team lost last weekend. I resent having to visit those distant relatives. I resent the credit card company demanding payment. I resent having to do this stupid exercise.* See if you can keep going to the point where it becomes ridiculous. You might even begin to laugh at your own powers of resentment. It's good to get some of them off your chest.

At another level, we all probably have much deeper resentments to people whom we feel have harmed us in our lives. There's the boss who won't promote us or give us the pay rise we wanted. There's the lover who left us for someone else. There's the schoolteacher who seemed to single us out when we were a kid. And beyond all of them, there are our parents who we found perhaps too controlling, distant, smothering or abandoning.

As adults, most of us don't want to point the finger of blame at our parents. It's time, we feel, to get on with our own lives. They did the best they could and we get on perfectly well with them. Well, at least until we have to visit them for Christmas or a family reunion, when they drive us utterly insane with the odd 'casual' remark like 'That's *so* typical of you' or 'Trust you to say that!'

BACK TO OUR ROOTS

This is exactly where we can start. We don't have to blame our parents, but we can look outside of ourselves to where some of our behaviour started. Think back to the behaviour patterns that you acknowledged for yourself, plus the ones that your friends might volunteer for you.

Being honest, which ones might you have learned from your parents? When I did this exercise, one of the first connections I made was a behaviour (pointed out by my friends) that involved a tendency to be aloof or withdrawn. They said my attention could wander and I was no longer 'there'. My father seemed to get on with everyone, and my mother was the life and soul of the party, so how could I have learned that from either of them?

Looking at it further, I saw that my father often 'withdrew' from me as a child because he would be tired when he came home from work and liked to sit down in front of the TV. I wanted to talk to him and tell him about my day; I wanted to be bounced up and down on his knee and tickled. 'How could you just watch boring old TV? I don't want you to watch TV,' I would complain. Though it was long ago and well buried, I could imagine that as a child I might have resented that.

However, it seemed perfectly normal to me and became a model for my behaviour in relationships.

I wouldn't watch TV or even read the newspapers, as I had to be different, but I just might read a self-help or psychology book, one that would expand my mind. Even going out to dinner with friends, my mind would be drifting off to some idea or other. I became a sponge for knowledge and so could often be found at their bookshelves rather than sitting down talking with them. Withdrawn, yes, I would have to admit that one. I certainly would not want to pass that one on to my children.

So now I have the connection between the present and the past. How can I break its hold on me? If I blame my father, and leave it at that, then I merely get myself off the hook. If I just blame myself, then I can feel even worse about my life, and nothing changes. But if I can build a healthy boundary between a pattern that I learned on one side, and who I really am on the other, then the pattern's hold on me will be broken.

What we need to do now is build a strong psychological barrier against those patterns that keep us acting in the same old ways.

RECOVERY MEANS BUILDING A HEALTHY BOUNDARY

Good fences make good neighbours.
ROBERT FROST

We need to exaggerate, to dramatise the sense of frustration we have with our own lives so that we are motivated to change. It was not enough for me to say, 'I'm slightly fed up with being withdrawn.' I had to remember the many relationships I had destroyed because I simply could not be present to the other person. The result had been my suffering. I then searched in my own memory for times when I felt so alone that I had cried. (The last time had been on my birthday three months before. I was very low then. Instead of having a birthday celebration, I was all alone in my room just after a blazing row with my girlfriend.) I started to write as the first stage of expression. 'I'm fed up with having to be withdrawn. I learned it from you, Dad, and now I'm giving it back to you. Remember all the times I wanted to play with you, and you said that this was your favourite TV programme. Well, look at me, I have needs, too. Now I have to watch all my relationships getting ruined because I thought it was completely normal behaviour to make myself unavailable.'

Ridiculous? This is meant to be an exaggeration, in order to get out any old charge that remains. I copied my father not just because it was normal but because of course I wanted him to pay attention to me. If he didn't give me attention for simply *being*, then I had to *do* something to earn his interest. I had to behave in a certain way. My young mind was thinking, below any conscious level: 'You, Dad, are there quietly watching TV. I'll just sit here quietly and read. We don't need to actually talk to each other. Now, if I act just like you, will you like me more?'

The reason I needed to say 'I'm giving it back to you' was to build a boundary wall between his behaviour and mine. This psychological barrier would then exist to mark me as separate from him, rather than being merged or tied into his behaviour.

We all swear that we will *never* become like our parents, especially when it comes to bringing up our own children. But again and again we suddenly find ourselves doing exactly what they did, even saying what they said, and, horror of horrors, for those of us who have become parents ourselves, saying or doing it to our children. This is the wake-up call for some, the moment they realise they have to do something. How come, despite our best intentions, we repeat history?

As adults we believe we have a great deal of freedom in how we choose to live. But of course as children, we needed not only our parents' and carers' attention, but also their unquestioning and unconditional love. We depended on them utterly to feel warmly protected by that love. Little by little, however, we noticed that they had other interests. We were not their only focus. Our primitive minds made some connections: 'As I *am* now is not enough for them to love me. So I must *do* something to win their love.' We all start copying their behaviours, their moods and their physical expressions. We listen to and learn both their spoken and unspoken messages. Because this adoption of patterns starts with a heartfelt sense that we are not getting enough love, Bob Hoffman called it the 'Negative Love Syndrome'.

Even Michelangelo felt the need to please his father. He wrote to him once, 'I am the most famous artist in the world . . . I have worked night and day and undergone hardships of every description . . . *but I still do not know what you want of me.*' This sense of almost desperate willingness to please stays with us because part of us is still locked in the past. Emotionally, we retain many of the characteristics of a child before our intellect was fully formed. Since the roots are emotional, we need to do something where we are emotionally engaged. In doing that, we can tear out the roots of these old patterns and truly be free to live our own lives.

The first step is to be aware that we are not *born* with a pattern. We learned it. The next step is to 'give it back' through healthy expression.

ANGER: ITS HEALTHY POWER

We are very frightened of anger and forget that many so-called primitive cultures use it to purify themselves and move on from the past. We grow up feeling that we're being bad if we're angry. Rather than being told it's a healthy expression of feeling, we are told 'Be quiet', 'Don't answer back', 'How dare you raise your voice to me', or finally, 'Go straight to your room. I'm having none of this'. Of course we learn to keep it inside. We brood, we pout, we imagine taking our revenge. Or, perhaps even more damagingly, we learn to turn it in on ourselves. We beat ourselves up and follow a path of self-destruction.

Ever since you learned to repress anger, it has built up inside you. If you can learn to express it, though, you will release yourself from its burden.

Buddha said that if you put an angry bull inside a barn, he will kick the doors down and harm himself. If you give him a big field, he will discharge his anger without hurting himself or anyone. That is our challenge.

Expressing anger is holy work. Anger often blocks us from connecting with our spiritual selves and our loved ones. By discharging it, we can reconnect with ourselves and our loved ones. If you think it's not holy work, consider how much of the time Jesus was angry in the New Testament. Anger allows a fire of change to spread through us, burning up years of old undergrowth in the forest. The Old Testament God is also not one to hold back on anger and there's a passage that says, 'Be angry, but do not sin. Let not the sun go down upon your wrath.' The real sin may be in keeping anger inside, letting it eat away at you and your life like a cancer.

I was angry with my friend.
I told my wrath, my wrath did end.

I was angry with my foe,
I told it not,
My wrath did grow.

William Blake. 'A Poison'd Tree'

TRACING THE PATTERNS
THAT CONTROL US

Have another look at the patterns you considered for yourself on pages 26 and 28. This time, though, keep in mind which of your parents might also have had that pattern. Is there a relationship between what they did and what you are doing?

Look for these connections between you and your parents. Was your mother a victim? Was your father a workaholic? Perhaps your stepfather was always running around helping everyone else, and never at home. Did you directly copy any of their patterns? That is the most direct way of learning a pattern; you adopt it. If, however, you needed to rebel to make a stand against them, think which of your patterns might have had its roots in rebellion. What opposite pattern might there have been in them? For example, you race around like a wannabe Formula One driver, not just ignoring speed limits but accelerating when you see those annoying signs. Your parents, on the other hand, always obeyed the exact speed limit, because it was their pattern to do everything to the precise letter of the law. You may think you're being different, but you are still tied in to them emotionally, held back by the past.

To make the link more clear, remember a family situation from your childhood where you might have been learning that pattern. See it as if it is happening at the present moment. That way your emotions and intellect become engaged in this enquiry. What is your mother or father saying or doing? Take, for example, the pattern: 'critical'. Your father is doing your homework with you and says: 'Look, you've done it wrong again. Trust you to mess it up.' How did you feel at the time? Make an emotional connection with that scene. Then think of a time when you have been critical recently. It could have been directed towards yourself or to someone you are close to. Again, remember how you felt right then. Allow both of the scenes to be clear in your mind and to have an emotional response. Why make the connection? So that you have the necessary charge to let go of the pattern. You have to know how much you dislike its hold on you before you can drop it with a deep commitment and life energy.

Next, write a short letter, imagining that you are that small child again telling your father that you don't want to take on his patterns. Let him know that it's his stuff, not yours.

When you feel the emotional charge in you has lessened or disappeared, burn the letter or crumple it up, squeezing it tightly between your hands before throwing it away.

The act of writing a letter detailing where you feel you have been wronged does not increase your anger. It allows expression for it so that it can move out of you.

After writing, check in to see if you feel that it's time to move on. Imagine there's a scanner passing through your body sensing whether there is an old emotional response to this issue. Ask yourself: 'Am I fed up with always blaming others (or myself)?'

Good girls don't confront

I tried persuading Carmen, a mousey mother of four, to express her old feelings about how her mother had played victim all the time. Carmen could not dream of saying or writing anything 'bad' about her mother. The problem was not just one of the past. She was incapable of confronting her husband about why he still kept seeing his 'ex' wife. Good girls do not confront, apparently. They simply learn to put up with anything, just as Carmen's mother did with her father.

I reminded Carmen that her real, physical mother would not hear her, while the higher, spiritual self of her mother would thank her for getting out the rage.

'But I still can't say those awful words to her.'

'OK, Carmen, you feel that you can't. But if you keep your rage so locked down it may have a side-effect. It means that you stay a victim in your relationship, doesn't it?

She glared at me in such a way that I knew I had found the right button. She then immediately picked up a pen and started writing. Thirty minutes later, she was still head-down, furiously scribbling a letter to her mother. She was well on the road to recovering her own power and self-esteem.

If the level of the emotional response is high, we call it a 'charge'. You can use a scanner or an imaginary 'charge meter' to measure how much work you need to do on a pattern. If there's not much charge, (and by now you can trust yourself for that to be true), then you may already have let it go, Don't force an issue that does not exist. But if the charge is strong, then scream your frustration into a pillow, or have a really good shout while you are in the car (don't worry, the other drivers will think you're singing along to a radio station). Let out how sick and tired you are of the pattern inside of you.

Take some minutes to breathe and imagine letting go of that pattern. Release it from your mind and from your body. Allow yourself to feel a sense of satisfaction.

HEALTHY EXPRESSION

Build a bigger picture of your family and the patterns you might have adopted as you were growing up. Who do you see yourself playing out these patterns with now in your current life – with your boss, lover, spouse, brother or sister?

How fed up are you? Write down what most pisses you off. Make it emotional! Get in touch with how tired of it you are: *I hate being such a goody-goody all the time! I really resent that everyone dumps on me. Why am I always the scapegoat?* Free up some of your energy.

Trace back the patterns. How did you learn them as a child, and from whom? Were you copying your mother or father or trying to rebel? In your mind, let this parent of your childhood know how much you want to be rid of this role or pattern. It's their stuff, not yours. Express it. Dump it. Keep going until the emotional charge inside is spent. You'll have the opportunity to forgive later on.

There is such a strong pressure in society not to express our anger that many, perhaps even most people, find it hard to let it out. A young journalist called Melinda felt that she would become as bad and violent as her own father if she screamed and shouted. Nothing has ever been gained by it, she claimed.

Indeed that was largely true. Anger was used by her father to intimidate and frighten the rest of the family. Anger is mainly used as a tool not for freedom but to keep people suppressed on a family, national and global level.

The opposite may be true for you. You may have grown up in a house where no one was *ever* allowed to get angry. As a result, anger was something placed outside the norms of the family book of rules. It would probably feel 'unnatural' to be openly angry when you grew up.

Think again of the possible effects of suppressed anger on your body. It could be that you get headaches, stomach-aches, or backaches. There has even been a link proven between anger and heart disease. Reflect on the effect of repressed anger on your life in general. It could be taking so much effort to keep your anger down, to de-press, that you yourself are depressed. It could be that in your relationships you criticise and wear others down rather than ever clearing the air. Or you become passively aggressive, claiming 'I'm not the one with the problem. You are.'

It could be that your anger comes out as sarcasm. You're so dissatisfied that you make comments that *seem* witty but are actually cruel. Of course, if anyone says you're being cruel, you reply, 'Look, I was only joking.'

A very common way of seeing old, 'historical' anger is in our driving habits. No longer are you the quiet, polite person of home and office. The thoughts in your head are ones specific to the open road: *My God, how can they let her out? Hey, why not park in the middle of the road? Get off my back! How dare you cut across me!* See how driving down the road becomes an analogy for unresolved life issues? We don't want anyone 'on our backs' like our mothers might have been. We don't want someone to cut across us, like our fathers might have done when we tried to speak. We may once again feel like a non-person, a second-class citizen, and store a lot of pent-up anger waiting for an outlet.

All of these incidents are examples of historical anger, a type that has far more charge than the situation calls for. Appropriate anger, on the other hand, is when you react to a real injustice. The reaction will be deserved and your anger acts as a catalyst for change. It shouts out, 'Enough!' and allows you to start putting a different course of events into action.

It's far better to find a safe place to let out your pent-up anger than to sit on top of it. When you've taken off the lid, you don't have to be angry at yourself or others. Instead, you'll have a great sense of calm and peace.

COMPLETING THE SECOND STEP OF THE PROCESS

By healthily expressing the issues of the past, you have helped to resolve them. They can no longer take over and use you. You have given them back. You do not have to copy or rebel against the behaviour you witnessed earlier in your life. You have far more freedom to be yourself.

Your own Spiritual self will always keep you moving towards that place of freedom. It reminds you that, 'Trust that there is enough love in the world. Trust that just as you are, you are loveable.'

You have the courage and the motivation to face what it is that you need to change. You have come far along the path now. You have looked with complete honesty at your patterns and built a boundary between them and you. You have examined your own patterns and your family history and, learning from the past, decided that you will not repeat old mistakes. You have released and discharged the old emotions that clothed those patterns. You have taken power back into your own hands.

Stay on this exciting journey of self-discovery. You will find on it greater aliveness and love at every step. Live fully in the joy of the present and you will be headed towards a wonderful future.

TASKS FOR THE DAY

Awareness: Take one of your major patterns today and examine it in all your actions and relationships. Try one that has become a main role, or lifestyle choice; for example, boss, victim, teacher, rescuer, know-it-all, martyr, blamer, pleaser, peacekeeper, black sheep. Treat the day as a play with this as your part. By playing out your role, and even exaggerating it, it becomes more obvious as a mask and therefore easier to let go. Repeat this exercise as many times as you wish.

Expression: You are aware of some of the most dominant patterns in your life. Now dump them in a letter, just as if you were collecting all the old garbage and throwing it in the bin. Write this letter to the parent you remember from your childhood (but never, ever send it). Tell them that you learned the patterns in the first place. 'You taught me to be such a perfectionist that I feel I have to do a perfect job! I can't even get started sometimes because you taught me if it wasn't done well, it wasn't worth doing at all . . .' Leave your cynical and judgmental mind behind, and remember, you are writing *not* to your physical parent, not to their loving side, but to their programmed dark side. Of course they have a wise, loving side. We will see much more of that later once the old resentments have been expressed

Express it through your body, your Physical self. Can you sense any blocked energy in your jaw, gut or back?

To what do you think it might relate? Do you need to dance or run it out? Get out of your chair, put on some loud music or your running shoes and *move*! Move it out of you.

Spend five minutes each day getting to know and listening to your Spiritual self.

5
Healing Your Past

To err is human, to forgive, divine.

Step Three: Forgiveness

It's time to move on from becoming *aware* and *expressing* what frustrates you or limits you. Now that we have established that patterns originally stem from our parents or carers, the next stage is let go of all blame and *forgive*. It's time to forgive them and of course yourself. It's time to move on from the past.

There needs to be a bridge built between psychotherapy's view of the world and the spiritual perspective. Therapy says that you have to go through the childhood pain and hurt. Spiritual traditions say that you have to transcend the negative and cultivate positive emotions such as love and forgiveness. Critics say that therapy is digging up old graves, while looking for the positive is merely a 'spiritual bypass'.

What if you did both? What if first you walked through the pain? You deal with the real or imagined hurts until the charge inside of you has gone. Then you turn your perspective around one hundred and eighty degrees and learn to feel love where before you might have felt anger or sadness.

But *how* do you jump from one to the other? The bridge

across the divide is built by first understanding how the pain and hurt caused by your parents and carers was not their choice. It was the only way they knew to behave. If you learned to be withdrawn or frightened by copying their behaviour, how do you think *they* in their turn learned it . . .? Exactly. They were also copying their parents.

As you know, intellectual awareness is not enough to move us profoundly. We need to understand *emotionally* so that old pain can be transformed to a clean space of let-go. Up to now, you have been tracing back your own patterns and seeing the family connection. By connecting the patterns to your parents and then writing a letter addressed to them, you were 'accusing' them of giving those patterns to you. For justice to be done, at some point you have to turn things around and 'defend' your parents, just as in a courtroom. This defence will enable you eventually to let go of any old blame. It need not be tied yet to a pardon. You are assembling the evidence, just as you did for the 'prosecution'. You can then decide. It may be that you have to go back and forth between prosecution and defence for a few rounds until all the evidence has been heard.

So after Awareness and Expression comes Forgiveness.

We do not get to forgiveness by clicking our fingers. It is hard work, and we do it in stages. First we learn to gently understand the background behind the actions. How did our parents grow up? What were they learning?

The Native Americans said that to really understand someone, you had to walk in their moccasins. This is exactly what we need to do to begin the journey of forgiveness. We need to walk with them through their childhood to understand emotionally their lives as vulnerable little children. The emotional understanding that this walk gives us will lead us into a softer heart and heal the fiery anger. Finally, when all steps have been taken, we will come to a place of deep letting go, of unconditional forgiveness.

The forgiveness is not only for parents who might have caused us pain in our lives, but also for ourselves. All of us have made mistakes, and all of us have led life at less than our full potential. We are all learning at different speeds and different levels.

Forgiveness does not imply that we are condoning the behaviour or letting someone off the hook. It means that we are strong enough to move on from the old grudge. As we said before, we can still condemn the action while seeing the being behind the behaviour. Each of us has a Spiritual self inside as well as a set of very human conditioned responses. By forgiving we bridge the gap to our own spiritual nature.

BUT IS IT THAT EASY?

True forgiveness is probably one of the hardest things to achieve as a human being because it means both acknowledging that we have been wronged by another person *and* understanding that it is better to let go for our sakes and theirs. For some of us it is easier just to 'forget about it' and get on with our lives, allowing the negative energy to subtly fester inside and be turned against us. For others, it becomes simpler to point the finger of blame at someone else rather than take the responsibility into our own hands to change things. It's the old syndrome of 'I'd rather be right than happy.' Bear in mind, though, that whenever you point one finger at someone else, there will be three fingers pointing back at you. Just look at your hand the next time you do the pointing.

Of course talking about forgiveness may be hard to swallow

for those victimised as children by adults who should have known better, or people who suffer cultural and religious oppression. However, we have a choice whether we bag up our hatred and vengeful feelings and sling them over our shoulder for the rest of our lives, or actively seek ways of healing those wounds so we can use our experiences to help others. We are all each others' teachers and students.

A huge change can occur when we forgive ourselves for letting someone else take advantage of our weaknesses, and so reclaim our personal power and integrity. In this moment of truth, we can let go of the pain of being 'wronged'. Something then happens in our hearts which is quite miraculous. We open a door deep inside our psyche to allow the poison to drain out, leaving us free to walk away from the situation with grace, humility and compassion for our aggressor as well as for ourselves. Remember how Nelson Mandela invited his jailer to his presidential inauguration? He set a fine example for a country that needed to forgive its past mistakes in order to build a brighter future.

In the words of an old teaching: 'The real hero is he who turns his enemy into his friend.'

When you do expressive work, you are able to feel a source of inner strength. In your mind, confronting your parents for what has been done to you gives you a healthy sense of boundary. 'You are over there, and I stand here.'

The next stage of your Process should be done very gently. To move yourself on from this stage of empowerment is delicate work. You need at all times to keep a balance between an inner Emotional self that may feel wounded and is only just beginning to feel its strength on one side, and on the other, the need for your Spiritual self to lead you further into growth by forgiving the past.

Martin Luther King put it this way: 'Forgiveness does not mean ignoring what has been done or putting a false label on an evil act. It means, rather, that the evil act no longer remains a barrier to the relationship.'

This is what this process of change does: it lets you come to a resolution with your parents so that you can move beyond having to act in the old programmed ways. You have heightened your awareness of the internalised negative or 'dark' side of your parents, which you have copied or rebelled against. You need to feel free of that by changing deeply, emotionally, how you hold those internalised images in your mind. You need to *understand* how your parents came to act that way, then to forgive them once and for all.

This understanding lies between two stages of the Process: between empowerment and letting go. It takes the pressure off the need to simply forgive. It also gives us the emotional depth to truly forgive.

'But I've already forgiven them,' you cry. So what's the point if you have already forgiven them in your own mind?

Many people do indeed feel they have already dealt with their past and have moved on from resentment to forgiveness. But Scott Peck, author of *A Road Less Traveled*, warns us about the dangers of doing this inner work by half-measures: 'A great many people suffer from the problem I have come to call "cheap forgiveness". They come for their first session with a therapist and say, "Well, I know that I didn't have the greatest of childhoods, but my parents did the best they could, and I've forgiven them." But as the therapist gets to know them, he finds that they have not forgiven their parents at all. They have simply convinced themselves that they have.'

Don't go for cheap forgiveness. Make an emotional investment and you will reap a huge emotional reward.

HOW DID MY MUM AND DAD LEARN TO BE THAT WAY?

You may have heard various stories about your parents' lives. You may have heard them tell you that life was good and that they had no problems with their parents. This could be true. On the other hand, if you had children, would you want to tell them how lonely and sad you sometimes felt as a child? Would you want to tell your children that their grandparents were not always so sweet and kind? No, you would probably cover up any old hurts you felt.

We may never know for sure how our parents grew up. It may even be harmful to ask them about their childhoods; they could shut down and become defensive: 'Why are you asking me this all of a sudden?' However, there is a way that we can find our way to an *emotional* truth about their own roles and patterns without scaring up old skeletons in the cupboard. This work is done in the sanctuary of our own minds.

Imagine that you are at the supermarket and you see a little boy who is standing alone in the aisle. His face is red with crying and you become concerned. You walk over, bend down and ask him what's wrong. He says, 'My mummy got cross with me and shouted. She said I had to stay here all on my own.' There's a pang in your heart as you feel for his pain.

Could you imagine your mother or father in that child's position? Have you *ever* thought of your Mum and Dad as weak and vulnerable, crying out for their Mum and Dad? Have you thought of how they felt setting off for their first day of school, or what they went through when they were told off? What if you were able to travel through time and spend hours and hours talking with the child that grew up to be your mother or father?

Perhaps this is the most original contribution of the Process.

It teaches us to see our parents as vulnerable souls and through that to find a new understanding for them. Feeling that, we can then forgive both in them and in ourselves (remembering we are carrying around our *internalised* parents) the faults that are all part of human nature. The way from an old self to a new positive self has to pass through a stage of understanding and forgiveness.

Mum and Dad were once little children too

The magic in this part of the process comes through taking a whole new perspective. You allow yourself to shift your viewpoint and see yourself with your parents before anything bad happened between them and you. It is a clean and honest relationship that can deliver a deep truth. A type of truth beyond the understanding of our normal minds. It's a truth that is derived from our hearts and our souls that have been crying out for deliverance from the wrongdoings of the past.

What is it that *you* would most like to know? What family tradition would it be great to let go of? Is it that relationships always dissolve, or that you and your family are not good at acknowledging feelings? Think of something that would motivate you to get a conversation going.

Do the following exercise when you know that you will not be disturbed or have to leave suddenly. Allow at least thirty minutes, and preferably one hour, for it to feel effective. Many people have found it useful to record on to a tape and then play it to themselves with their eyes closed. Quiet music is also useful in the background to relax our bodies and our minds.

LISTENING TO UNDERSTAND

Imagine that you're back in your sanctuary, a place of great natural beauty. See yourself there, with the sun shining down. It's as if you can even feel yourself being warmed by that sunshine. There may be a slight breeze around you. You smell how wonderfully fresh the air is with its scent of flowers. You feel relaxed and totally at ease.

You are feeling very rested, safe, and at peace with yourself. You walk around and find a tree to sit by. The grass around it is wonderfully soft. Take a few deeper breaths, letting yourself relax even more. Now, from your present age, let yourself count back the years until you feel yourself as a child, around the age of twelve or thirteen. Do you remember how you looked at that time? You are curious and willing to learn more about life. Now you see coming up to you another child, a girl who is also around twelve or thirteen. She sits down next to you and you know right away that it's your mother as a child.

You spend the first couple of minutes just looking at each other. Allow your critical intellect to be quiet. Then, in your mind, start talking to this girl, telling her that there's no need for her to be frightened of you. Make her feel comfortable. You would like to know more about her childhood. When you feel that there is some trust between you, ask your first question. 'What was it like growing up for you?' She may answer in general terms. Encourage her by asking a specific question. 'Were you frightened of your mother or father? How did they treat you?' Listen closely as she gives a response.

Ask another question when you are ready. Again, listen

to her answer. Continue by asking as many questions as you want. Make sure you cover the patterns of behaviour that you have already identified as coming from her.

Either now or in another sitting, do this exercise with your father and any other people who were significant in your upbringing and from whom you learned patterns.

When I first did this, I was sceptical. No, that's a lie. I was downright dismissive about this exercise. I thought that someone must have really lost the plot to come up with this one. I could see the need to list my *own* patterns. I could even do the work of expressing my old resentment about how I had grown up. But now here I was, an educated man, imagining talking to the child that grew up to become my mother. What was the man on when he dreamed this one up? Thank heavens no one was watching me!

Doing this work in my mind's sanctuary, I began to get – from my mother as a child – answers to questions that I had long held. I wanted to find out the origins of my mother's general anxiety, the free-floating variety that could be attached to any passing cause, no matter how unjustified. Where might that have come from? She said that her father was a gambler, addicted to horse-racing, and that the family constantly lived in fear of losing everything. Delving deeper, I asked her why she always seemed worried about what others thought? 'She' told me that her mother was obsessed by the opinions of others. My grandmother was very insecure about her place in society and passed it on to my mother. The little girl, my mother, always had to get her mother's approval for what she was wearing before going out to play with her friends. 'You can't possibly go out wearing that!' was one of her mother's often-used expressions. 'Whatever would the neighbours think?' Even the curtains had to fit in with local norms. 'Mind your manners' was heard every day. She could not just be herself, but had to fashion herself into someone else's idea of who she should be. Small wonder that I, Tim, as a teenager had become such a rebel, throwing all those lessons away to gain any sense of my own identity.

I was also particularly interested in the family tradition of guilt. In this imaginary dialogue, she told me about how as a child she was blamed for everything. Being the eldest, she was expected to *know* what to do. Her father was away working most of the time, so her mother was often lonely and bitter, taking her frustration out on my mother. She grew up watching out for the next torrent of blame. She was the scapegoat, and inevitably turned out to be the naughty one. 'If that's how you see me, that's what I'll become' her young mind had said. I began to feel a real softness for this vulnerable child who grew up to become my mother.

I myself have big issues about being abandoned and as a result grew up learning to be completely self-reliant. 'I don't need anyone' was my mantra. I know that my mother, like me, has an ambivalent attitude towards being in a relationship. I began to probe gently at this complex area. If I could ask the child inside of her how she felt about people, might that answer some of my confusion about how needy or how dependent I truly was beneath my confident exterior? She told me that she always felt insecure. Her parents had stayed together, but neither was ever really available to her. The emptiness she felt inside was never filled by them. In this imaginary realm, she told me how night after night they went out, leaving her to cry herself to sleep. At mealtimes they were more interested in her manners than her conversation or her feelings. I was moved by her story, and at times felt that I was really living inside her past.

My father, on the few occasions that I ever asked him in person, insisted that he had had a perfect childhood. Most people found him extremely easy to get on with, and he had no grievances with anyone. However, get him warmed up and he would utter the most outrageously unpolitically correct comments. It drove me insane and became a huge gulf between us both as a child and as an adult. How the Left Wing, the 'Loony Lefties' were trying to ruin the country and how evil they were was a favourite dinner party piece of his. I wanted to know how he became so black-and-white in his thinking.

Speaking to his imagined child of twelve, I learned about the pain he had never wanted to show or even talk about. His father was a very senior officer in the Navy, used to commanding thousands of people. When the Admiral came home, he ran his own house like a ship. As a child, my father could not question the commands of his father. At dinner he had to sit at the table and listen to his father declaiming about what was wrong with the world – inevitably with 'negative love'. By copying his father to earn his love, my father became rigid in his own beliefs.

I asked the child of twelve to let me know how he felt in his home, and he finally showed me his vulnerability inside. I felt for his pain and his loneliness as I never had before. There were times when he had cried himself to sleep, times when he had been hit or shouted at, times when he had to 'be brave' and bottle up his feelings. I saw a side of him I had never thought existed, and it changed our relationship hugely while he was still alive.

Many people to whom I have spoken said that it changed their view of their parents, even if they were already dead. It healed the past and freed them all to go their own ways.

But is it true?

What is happening during this exercise? Are we seeing the truth? We may never know for sure if we are finding out the truth or not while in this imaginary realm. Does it matter if it is objective truth or not? The point of this work is that its end justifies the means, and the end is to come to our own emotional truth. It's a truth beyond our ordinary understanding, one which allows our past to settle so that we can live in the present.

Defending our parents

Lisa Wenger and her brother Mike, who founded the Hoffman Institute in Italy, were talking one day about their experience of this work to understand and 'defend' our parents. They found that time and time again they had come across the same emotional truth in looking at the childhoods of both their parents, even if the actual scenes were not the same. They both saw their father as feeling very small and worthless compared to his two older sisters, and were very able to sympathise with his pain. But in one instance they came across an extraordinary similarity.

Lisa had been imagining the dialogue between the child of her mother and herself as a child. She wanted specifically to know how her mother had developed a pattern of feeling excluded. What she 'saw' was her mother trying to get the attention of her father, a Jungian analyst, again and again while he was sitting in a big armchair. It was a hopeless task, as he was buried in his scientific papers. She asked Mike what he had found out about this pattern of feeling excluded. He had done the dialogue work a few months earlier and, it turned out, had the same image of his mother trying to talk to her father in a big armchair and getting no reply. When they asked their mother about it, she said, 'But that's extraordinary. That's exactly what would happen. Every day when he came home, he took out paperwork from his briefcase and would sit behind them in a big red armchair. I could not even get an answer from him.'

A couple of years later, they were teaching a course together. At the point where they were explaining how to do this dialogue work, a woman in her fifties stood up and cried out excitedly, 'Now I know why my son came and asked me about a painting I had as a child.'

'What do you mean?' asked Lisa

'Well, when Paolo came home from doing the Hoffman Process, he asked me if I had a picture of a dog above my bed when I was a little girl. I had forgotten all about it, but yes, there was a picture of a dog, a lovely St Bernard, all the time I was growing up. I had asked him how he knew about it but he just smiled and said it was something that came into his mind.'

At that point, Lisa said, everyone who was listening gasped in astonishment. They were very content afterwards to go and do this work of the 'imagination' and let go of the scepticism they had felt beforehand.

DIALOGUE WITH PARENTS

Take a few of your patterns that you have already traced back to one of your parents. If they are ones with a lot of old energy attached, make sure you have managed to express the charge through bashing a pillow or screaming, running or dancing. When you have felt letting go, then choose a quiet time and a safe place. Choose one parent or carer.

Start by relaxing your body. Take a few deep breaths. Imagine yourself stepping onto a lift and going down seven levels. The lift stops, the doors open, and you find your-self back in your sanctuary at the age of about twelve. You walk around and come to a favourite tree. Sit down there and make yourself comfortable.

Imagine that, approaching you is the child of your mother or father around the age of twelve. Invite them to sit down opposite your child, here in your sanctuary, and slowly begin to ask questions in a very open way. Be careful not to make them defensive. Tell them you are here to learn and understand, not to blame. Listen to what they have to say. If you feel you're making it up, fine. Listen anyway. When you have heard it all, write it down. It's perhaps only when you read it again that you'll be funda-mentally touched by what you 'found out'. Let the emotional truth connect you with their vulnerability and the fact that they learned to act the way they did for a reason. They had no choice when they were children.

By holding this conversation with your 'child' parent, you arrive at a new level of heartfelt understanding about yourself and your family patterns. At this level you can undo the hold of the past by seeing them as vulnerable beings. In addition to this, you are calming the fire of anger that has burned during the expressive stage.

The healing that comes from this stage of the work occurs subtly and deeply. You are performing a type of psychic archae-ology, with yourself doing the gentle excavation. When you have completed the search, you are in position to go to the next stage, that of real forgiveness. There you perform a soft 'psychic surgery' on your heart and connect even more fully with your spiritual self.

You have softened yourself in order to heal and move on.

6

Making Peace and Moving Forward

There is but one freedom, to put oneself right before death. After that, everything is possible.

ALBERT CAMUS

Understanding that both you and your parents did not have a choice in your emotional education allows you to reach a tender place of acceptance. That is an important part of the journey of forgiveness, but it is not the end of the road. You have to go further into your heart if you want to meet them on an equal level, in what the Sufi mystic Rumi called 'a field beyond right and wrong'.

The next step of the process, therefore, is to move into true Forgiveness with compassion. Why? The overall aim is to see people as equals and to free you of the grip of the past. Parents, carers and other figures from the past can then no longer reach out and control your reactions in the present. Remember, this is all in the internal workings of your mind. How you learn to view your parents and carers becomes a template for how you view other important people in your life. It may be that you have become stuck in fear or resentment or resignation towards your parents. When you are able to cut the negative cords with them, you set both them and yourself free from old, tired reactions. As a result, you will be truly able to start living your life for you, free and unburdened. You will be able to make profound changes in the very core of your being and in every aspect of your life.

Forgiveness means closing a chapter and moving on.

RITUAL FORGIVENESS

To get to this stage, where you will reach a deep level of compassion, you need to do something out of the ordinary. You need a ritual to move from your everyday world to one where you are in a more profound level of consciousness. Doing this, you imprint on your mind a powerful memory that the past is over and that you do not have to go back there again and again. It's over, and you can walk away from it with a clear heart.

You need to give yourself the opportunity to say goodbye to the dark or negative side of your parents. This is the side that caused the hurt, humiliation and pain, because of their own wounds, which were inherited from their upbringing. At this time, you can also pay homage and respect to the spiritual selves of your parents, so that they may find peace within their own souls. You can of course use this ceremony to grieve for parents and carers who may have died, and to put to rest any issues that have been unresolved.

You can do this in a number of ways. One that we have found to be most effective is to light a candle for each of them; imagine that you are speaking to them from deep within your heart, forgiving them for all that has gone on in the past. Do this in a space that you consider sacred, whether a part of the house, a church, or outside in nature's beauty. Collect a photo or two of each parent, and a memento of theirs. This could be something like a piece of jewellery, a favourite book, or a letter that they sent you. Arrange them in front of you, as if you were making an altar, alongside the candle. Sit comfortably and allow yourself to meditate for a few minutes, looking over their things and being reminded of all your parents did in their lives. Make sure that you voice their positive achievements as well as what they may have suffered in their lives, mentioning some of the attributes that you received that have served you well.

Once you have done this inner work we encourage you to visit your parents in person and unconditionally express your love towards them. This could be the first time in their lives or yours that this has been said, and has the chance therefore of being a powerful emotional memory. This healing is of a spiritual nature and enables such a deep sense of connection to take place that a powerful cleansing may occur.

No longer a prisoner

Have you ever heard the song that goes:

> *Every generation blames the one before,*
> *And all of their frustrations come beating*
> *on your door.*

I know that I'm a prisoner
to all my father held so dear,
I know that I'm a hostage
To his hopes and fears.

I just wish I could have told him
In the living years.

It's too late, when we die,
To admit we don't see eye to eye

Mike and the Mechanics, 'The Living Years'

I had heard the song many times before, one day, doing some work around the house with the radio on in the background, I really was hit by the meaning of the words. They were wonderfully simple and touching, reminding me of how we live blindly, usually only realising too late what it is that we need to clean up. What, I asked myself at that point, if *my* father was to die before I made my peace with him? How would I feel living the rest of my life with old hurts and fears still in the air? What if my own children were to grow up with an old energy of hurt and blame around them?

When I finished university, I left the country without saying good-bye to my parents or thanking them for my education. I got a series of dead-end jobs that must have upset them deeply. Years went by when I would not visit them, or even call to ask how they were and give them my news. There was still a victim child in me shouting back, 'See how you like it.'

When we act, consciously or unconsciously to get back at our parents, we end up hurting ourselves. The desire for revenge and vindictiveness is always a two-headed monster, and one head turns back to bite itself. Of course, I felt totally dissatisfied emotionally, intellectually and spiritually by these jobs. I was a far cry from being the 'flaming torch' that George Bernard Shaw said we might be.

Forgiving my parents was an act of kindness not only to them, but also to myself. I wanted to put the past behind and choose an adult life full of new and exciting responses rather than continuing with my old and worn-out way of doing things.

So it was that many years and many dreadful jobs later, I made arrangements to travel back and make my peace with my parents.

I met my father first on the edge of the Serpentine lake in London's Hyde Park. It was a place that held many sweet memories of childhood for me.

After a few minutes catching up with each other, I drew my chair closer towards him and asked for his hands. He looked puzzled, but gave them to me, and I held them in mine. I then looked him in the eye and said, quietly but clearly enough for him to hear, words from the depths of my heart: 'Dad, I just want to say, I love you.' He appeared at first not quite to understand, but then I saw his expression change as his face softened. A tear came into his eye as he took in not just the words, which had never passed between us before, but also the feeling in my heart that had made those words possible.

He was very moved, so much so that he was not able to say anything for a while, but then he looked closer at me and, squeezing *my* hands said, 'I love you, too, and I always have.'

That, of course, did it for me, and the tears leapt into my eyes. So there we were, two grown men in the centre of a big city, crying. Years of misunderstandings were washed away right then.

Our relationship changed dramatically from that day.

Whenever I visited or called, our conversations were no longer limited to the two or three safe topics that had been our domain up until then (the news, movies and the price of property). We built up a friendship as two human beings who shared the strongest physical resemblance, as well as a whole load of inherited behavioural patterns.

Don't put it off if you want to get clear. Remember: *it's too late, when we die, to admit we don't see eye to eye.*

A word of warning

If you do feel you have leftover stuff to process with your parents, be very careful about doing it directly with them. If you go to them, go with a loving message. Often, people who have told their parents about how they suffered as children are retraumatised. Their mothers and fathers don't want to acknowledge any mistakes, so they either deny them totally or admit them, saying yes, but you deserved it because you were an absolutely horrible child.

The healthy response for a parent would be to admit mistakes and apologise. If *your* child comes up and accuses you of something, or asks for clarity about what happened, say – if it is true – that you made a mistake but that you did not intend them any harm. Let them see that you are a human being with feelings as well. We have all tried our best to be good parents and we're all still learning.

Parenting is a very sensitive issue in this society. Hint at a less than happy childhood, and it may sound like you are accusing your parents of abuse. Tread carefully here. Society at large does not want to admit it may be mistreating its children.

Driven by rage

Grant had a huge amount of anger inside. The one pattern driving all his behaviour was 'rage'. When I first met him, his face was a livid shade of red. Given that he was also a very large and well-built man, most people were frightened of him and gave him a wide berth. His eyes conveyed the message: 'Don't mess with me' while his body always looked like it was poised to strike.

As a child, Grant had been picked upon by his father, and considered to be the bad apple in the family. Whatever went wrong, he was blamed. Almost every night, he had been whipped with a belt to reinforce the message. Grant's attitude to the world was formed to protect himself, day after day, from being hurt not just physically but also in his heart. He was a very lonely and self-protected man of forty.

Grant had not seen his father for fourteen years, following a violent argument. Even though they were never close, they had at one time started a construction company together, in order to make some money. Grant had been feeling for a while that his father was taking too high a salary, considering he was not actively participating. Grant felt taken advantage of, just like a child, and asked his father to accept less. His Dad said, 'No, you ungrateful bastard. You'd be nothing without me.' Grant lost it, called his father some names and told him to get the hell out of the office. Which is what his father did. He went straight to the bank, cleaned the account out, and never said another word to Grant.

Now, fourteen years later, Grant was being encouraged by his circle of friends to go and make up with his father. They were all involved in a personal development support group that met twice a month. He put it off and put it off. His friends could see that he needed to break the chains that were still tying him to his father, even though they never spoke, met or even saw each other. Those chains were formed of hate and rage and were dragging Grant's life force down and down.

Grant finally heard the truth when one of his friends said, 'You'll never be free until you can give your father unconditional love and forgive what he did to you. Until you do that, you'll be tied to the past, dredging up the old memories to make you feel bad.'

Grant called his mother, not his father, and told her that he would be coming up, but not to let his Dad know yet. He didn't want his father to veto his visit before he had a chance to show that things really had changed with him. He drove up there on a cold winter's day with his heart thumping all the way.

Grant walked in that Saturday morning while his father was reading the paper. 'Well, well, well,' said his father. 'Look what the cat brought in.'

Grant sat down in a chair right next to his father and looked him softly in the eye.

'Dad, I'm not here to pick an argument. I want to say that I'm sorry for all the hurt I caused you. I want to say that beyond everything that has happened between us in the past, I love you.'

'What?'

'I love you.'

Silence. His father took a deep breath.

'Goodness me, Grant. I don't know what to say. What's happened to you?'

'Well, Dad, I started feeling that life was too short for us to still be enemies. I wanted to make up. From my side, I'm clear. I made some mistakes, I acted out of anger, and I ask you to understand that and, if you can find it in your heart, to forgive me.'

His father looked at him and tears came to his eyes.

'Oh, God, Grant, you have no idea what this means to me. I've waited so long for this.' Then the tears started to flood down his cheeks. Grant pulled his chair closer and hugged this old man, his father. He joined him in crying as well.

Grant came and told me that since then, he has felt free as never before. His face now has a healthy complexion and his eyes have a much gentler look. Something deep must have shifted because people are no longer frightened of him. 'My other partner at work jokes that I might be getting too soft, though, but I'm fine with that.'

MAKING PEACE WITH OTHERS IN YOUR LIFE

If you feel that you may be caught in an unresolved issue that is still causing you pain or grief, it is important to go through some kind of ritual that can help you to put this to rest. You may want to do this on your own, or with someone you trust, who can bear witness to your willingness to let go of the past.

The ritual that we use for parents can be adapted for anyone in your life you need to let go. Go into nature and choose a tree to symbolise someone who has died, or perhaps to say farewell to a relationship or to some kind of situation that you want to make peace with. You can either bury something beneath it which symbolically represents your willingness to resolve any emotional conflict, or to place a flower at the base of the tree. Alternatively you can simply light a candle at home.

Whatever you choose to do, imagine that you are talking to the spirit of the person with whom you feel aggrieved, or are mourning, and allow your feelings to surface. In doing so you can lay the past to rest. If tears come, let them flow. Tears allow us to let go of our grief and encourage healing to take place. Hold something soft to your chest, such as a pillow or a jumper. This provides a comfort, something to weep into. You might find yourself rocking backwards and forwards, allowing emotions to move up from deep within your body and soul.

When you feel ready, ask the person who you are wishing to make peace with for forgiveness and, if appropriate, grant them yours. Absolve them of any blame, and then *let them go*, as long as this does not cause them any harm. It is through actively demonstrating this kind of willingness to forgive that we can finally acknowledge intellectually *and* emotionally that it is time to move forward with our own lives. It allows us to develop a mature sense of compassion for ourselves as well as for others. After you have finished, make a vow to yourself about how you are going to live your life in a space of love and self-acceptance from this day on – a vow that means something to you and one that you are committed to carrying out.

Extraordinary things can occur when we do ritual work such as this. It is as if the veil between the seen and unseen worlds becomes thin, and miracles take place.

Learning how to forgive allowed me to undo the message about having to be right. Throughout my life, my older brother Justin was always the one getting into trouble. He had to be bailed out of jail a few times and once even had to be rescued from India where he had 'lost' his passport. He may well have sold it to get drugs. My family feared his phone calls as they usually meant another crisis. I became so frustrated with him and the worry he caused all the family, that I decided to break off contact with him.

Years later, I felt an overpowering wish to reconcile with

him. In my mind, whatever he had done was worth forgiving if I was to have a relationship with him. After all, he was the person closest to me – my only full brother. We were 'Irish twins' with less than a year's age difference between us. A voice inside me was saying, 'He is OK just as he is. I cannot nor do I want to judge him anymore.' When I met him again, having not seen him for a number of years, I let him know exactly what was going on in my heart. We were able to talk to each other as never before. We finally were able to let go of the past and love each other again.

TASK FOR THE DAY

With whom do you need to find forgiveness? Who are the old lovers, partners, teachers, people in your life with whom you have played a role that has left some kind of karmic debt? It's too late, when you die, to deal with unfinished business. Do it now.

Then take the following steps:

- Become aware of your grievance first, then write out any old pain.
- If you need some physical expression of it, dance or shout it out. Then breathe soft light into your heart.
- Imagine this person as a small child, and ask them how they learned to be so hurtful or unkind.
- Devise your own ritual to express your compassionate forgiveness. Let them go. If appropriate, go and forgive or ask forgiveness in person. Atone for what has happened between you in the past. Find the true meaning of the word: 'at-one-ment'.

FORGIVING YOURSELF
FOR PAST MISTAKES

We learn to forgive others, but often we forget to turn that back on ourselves. The ability to forgive ourselves is one of the most precious gifts we can ever receive. All of us make mistakes – the man, Einstein said, who never made any mistakes, never learned anything new. To forgive ourselves for these mistakes is to free ourselves and so be able to take new steps on our journey of inner growth.

Each time you forgive yourself you are learning to love and accept yourself more.

Begin by examining what is still really bothering you. Not the little things that happen in daily life, but the things that we regret ever happened. They may have been plaguing us with guilt ever since and draining our energy. It works more profoundly if you manage to feel the emotions that are triggered *and* let them pass through you. Make sure that you are not simply burying them again. If you feel you cannot do this alone, postpone it until you have someone you trust close to you. There may be great shame, or fear attached, so come to this exercise with care and sensitivity.

Make a list of mistakes you have made and finish by writing after each one, 'And I forgive myself'. Use a separate piece of paper so that you can ritually burn it afterwards.

Guilt of an affair

Jenny had long been nursing guilt from a brief affair she had had. It had happened while her husband had been away for many months and she had felt lonely and neglected. As a result, she had taken her affection for him out of the marriage and found it hard to bring back. She had also lost her self-respect because of breaking the vows she had sworn to uphold. Since she had come to a forgiveness for her parents first she had learned *emotionally* the power of forgiveness. She knew that she could not continue beating herself up, and so she talked about this with an understanding friend. Her friend encouraged her to see it as a mistake which she could learn from, forgive herself for and then move on.

Jenny wrote the story of her affair from beginning to end. As she wrote it she realised that she had been looking for love, just as she had as a child. One night when she had finished it, she picked up the story, found a scarf that the man had once given her, and went outside to the bottom of her garden. She made a fire, burning the story on it. Looking at the flames, she said to herself, 'It's over. I forgive myself.' Then she dug a hole and buried the scarf. Finally she looked up at the stars and realised how much more of life awaited her.

We have learned to let go of the past by forgiving the mistakes our parents, loved ones and we ourselves have made. We have given ourselves a fresh start in life. Now we are able to listen to our own present day reality, rather than being driven by the past.

We are now ready to understand and reconcile the differences between our emotional and intellectual selves.

7

Ending the Battle Between Your Emotions and Your Thoughts

Only a peace between equals can last.
WOODROW WILSON

Up until now, you have been looking long and hard at the patterns you acquired while growing up. You became aware of them, expressed any old charge around them, and then went on to wipe the slate clean through forgiveness. You have started living your life for *you*, with responses designed for the present moment rather than reactions set in the past. You have completed the work with your parents. So what possibly could there be left to work on? Well, to really live in the present with a deep sense of inner calm, we need to look beyond our parents and family background. After all, there are certain issues we have with nobody else but ourselves.

It's time now to move on and to look at the everyday conflict, not between you and anyone else, but between two very different aspects of your own mind – your feeling versus your thinking side. If there's a battle going on between the two, and you resolve this battle, then you will have peace of mind. You will have an even stronger foundation on which to build changes into your life.

Over many centuries, this battle has been portrayed in a variety of ways – Logic versus Emotion, the Greek god Apollo versus Dionysus, or Rational Man versus Intuitive Woman. In some countries, Descartes reigns supreme: 'I think, therefore I am', while his modern-day detractors respond, 'You think too much, therefore you can't feel!' The whole debate has come much more to the forefront recently with a widespread interest in Emotional Intelligence. In terms of the model we use for understanding human behaviour, the Quadrinity model with its four aspects of being, we are looking here at the two programmed parts of the mind, our Emotional and Intellectual selves.

Consider the following situations and see if any sound familiar.

THREE SCENES FROM EVERYDAY LIFE

Scene 1

You're about to stand up and make a presentation in front of some people from your company. Just before you do so, you notice that your heart is racing, the room suddenly feels over-heated and you need a drink of water. There's even some tight-ness in your leg muscles, the ones that would help you run away if, say, a sabre-toothed tiger was about to grab a bite of you.

Wait a moment! How come fear is taking over? You know your subject inside out. It's not fair. You're really good at what you do, and now you're about to be seen as a nervous newcomer. It's as if a time machine whisked you back to some nightmare classroom and you've been singled out to stand up and take your punishment.

Your well-trained rational mind has been preparing this presentation for weeks. You've even laid on some lovely charts and diagrams that will wow this jaded audience. How can you be let down by your body in this way?

It's not your body. It's your emotions that have hijacked you. The sweaty palms and leather mouth are due to an emotional response, the fear of being seen and of being criticised. The rational part of you begins with encouragement: 'I know I can do this.' But that doesn't help, so your mind starts getting tougher. You begin to talk to yourself like an impatient adult would to a child: 'Get a grip on yourself. Don't be so pathetic.' Even that doesn't seem to work. You feel consumed by fear. It gets so bad that you drop your notes on the way to the podium. When you're finally facing your audience, your mind seems scrambled. You read the outline in front of you, but it doesn't make sense anymore.

The audience doesn't want to criticise you, but they have come to hear you because they know you have skills that they would love to have. The voices of criticism are within – you have become your own worst enemy.

Scene 2

'Go on, call him,' your friends beg you. 'We know that he really likes you. And you like him, don't you?'

That's the problem. You *do* like him, and so the stakes are higher. 'What if I call him and he's very cool to me? He might think I'm really desperate. What if he told me that he didn't want to go out with me? I would be worse off than now. No, better that I don't call him in the first place. I'll wait until he makes the first move.'

Again, your emotions have hijacked you. You fear being rejected so much that you won't put yourself on the line. You torture yourself with wanting to call and not daring to. So you tell yourself that it's far better to leave things nice and safe. You're stuck where you have always been.

Scene 3

You're the boss. You're facing a team meeting. Your company is fairly progressive. It encourages people to be open and put things on the table. But as you think about the meeting coming up, your mind dwells on the people you think want to stab you in the back. Yes, you're convinced that they're going to unite and fight against you. You imagine all the grievances they've been storing up for months. They're probably going to criticise you for being impatient, expecting things to be always done in a certain way, and done by yesterday. Your communication style is one-way: 'Do this because I said so.' Oh no, you've become the nightmare boss.

'But wait,' you tell yourself, 'they don't appreciate me! They don't see how well paid they are, and besides, look at our rivals, that other company where they expect them to work evenings and weekends as well! They don't realise how lucky they are. Goodness, if I was such a bad boss I'd never give them any compliments. It was only last week, or certainly within the last month, that I went up to someone and told them they were doing really well. What do they want? Someone holding their hand telling them how fantastic they are all day long?'

Nice turn around! Here you've set yourself up as the victim. You've had an attack of the 'poor me's'. Better by far to be 'misunderstood victim' than 'wicked boss'.

AWARENESS OF TWO INNER ASPECTS: EMOTIONS AND INTELLECT

In each of these scenes, there's a battle going on between two parts of you. One part is rooted in the old brain, where the emotional responses lie. It matters little whether you are responding to something that is happening now, or to something that happened years ago. These old emotions have the power to flood your body and rational response. This is why you feel fear even though you *know* what you're talking about. It's why you never pick up the phone even though you know you won't get turned down. It makes you feel misunderstood even before you listen to the opinions of others. We call this part the Emotional self.

The other part of you is the more rational mind trying to make sense of the situation. It sifts information, trying to work out what is real and present from what is imagined and in the past. However, it is hampered by the shortcomings of the Emotional self, like a horse with a rope tied around its legs. We call this rational part the Intellectual self.

Over the years, your Intellectual self gives way little by little to impatience and frustration. Just as you sometimes simply give up on a tiresome colleague or family member, you also learn to shut down to messages from your Emotional self. That part still wants to act like a fearful or victimised child, but you're now living in the 'real' world of adults, and time is simply too short.

The problem is, the old reactions of the Emotional self are not just going to die or go away. They are living in you, waiting to pounce when the pressure is on and the stakes have been raised. So how have we learned to quiet our minds and live with ourselves? The answer is simple – by switching off. For some of us, drink has helped. Drugs might have done it for a while. Antidepressants, such as those in the Prozac family, serve for many to tranquillise the voices in our head that say: 'I can't cope with life.' Focusing on work tricks us for a while, until we collapse exhausted or find out that the financial compensation doesn't help us feel any better. Money really can't buy us love.

In this chapter, you will work with both these aspects – Emotional and Intellectual – in order to fully express and resolve their 'voices'. For that, we need to become more aware of how each side reacts in your day-to-day life.

Do you consider yourself to be mainly driven by your thoughts or by your feelings? Both, you may say. Well, think of yourself in an argument with a loved one. Do you rely on logic to persuade or do you often 'lose' it, giving your view of the matter amid shouts or tears?

Getting to know our emotional selves

Consider how you are in stressful situations. What happens to you on an emotional, feeling level? Do you lose your temper? Do you sit on your feelings, getting more and more withdrawn and shut down, but all the time storing up resentment? Do you play the 'victim' card, or the 'special one' needing lots of attention? The weekend comes and you've had a really bad week. How do you indulge your feeling side if you're down? A long credit card-fuelled trip to the shopping mall? Rushing around to see all your friends? Curling up in bed and having a marathon video session?

Are you becoming clearer about your emotional reactions when stressed? Make a written note of them if you like. Keep these in mind and we will use them later when we come to Expression.

To continue your journey back to yourself, you need to crawl back inside the emotional part of your being. Imagine it as a child of around eight years old. It's old enough to know about manipulation and game-playing, but still young enough to play 'victim' and 'poor me'. At this age lies the origin of the reactions of our Emotional self, an aspect that many people refer to as their 'inner child'.

Do you have any pictures or photos of yourself as a child? If you do, dig one out, look through the photo albums or ask your parents to send you some. Find one where you are about eight years old. What do you see in your child's face? Imagine the feelings that you had as a child – happy, vulnerable, alive, withdrawn, excited, pouting, fun loving, needy or frightened. Now imagine that this emotional aspect is still living inside you, the grown-up man or woman. You are *still* alive, spontaneous, creative and fun loving. And yet you are still carrying around a part that is withdrawn, a side that pouts, a person who is needy and frightened. This side of you is just more subtle and better-controlled now that you are grown up. When you feel put upon, you don't say, 'No, I won't do that.' Instead you deflect it and say, 'I'll get round to that later' or 'I'm really busy right now.'

We have to recognise that there is now an emotional part of us that is negatively programmed. If we can get to this emotional part and balance its needs and its voice with that of our rational side, then we can achieve a peace that deepens the one we already found with our parents. We can end the chattering monkeys in our own head, the ones some have called the 'shitty committee'.

Getting to know our intellectual selves

It may be that most of the time your rational side is in control. We often call this part of our minds the Adult Intellect, to distinguish it from the childlike Emotional self. Think of it as an image of yourself dressed just as you are today. You look exactly the same as you appear to the world now. Imagine this part of you standing in front of your body, right here.

What is this part of you doing or saying most of the time? What is its agenda? What does it see as its purpose? Does it want to control and be the boss? Does it mean to turn people off by its arrogance or sarcasm?

Listen closely as if you're listening to an old friend. When you feel more comfortable, ask some questions: 'Why are you so critical? Why do you have to control everything? Why is it so hard for you to relax?'

If you went up and said directly to someone, 'You're really argumentative, aren't you?' that person would most probably shut down and get defensive. But if you went up and said, 'Your intellect loves an argument, doesn't it?' they might just be curious to ask what you meant. You have the basis for a discussion. It's the same principal within yourself. You are encouraging yourself to stay open by bringing outside what is inside. You are 'externalising' a part of you. Simple, but effective.

So what do you habitually do when things are not going your way? Not the emotional response, but the one in your head. Do you analyse everything before making a move? Do you criticise others and run them down in your own mind? Do you rationalise an action, even if you feel deep down it was your mistake in the first place? Do you talk a subject to death? Think of some of the over-rational reactions you have under stress. Jot them down if you like. Again, we'll be using these later when we come to Expression.

Remember, when you are considering the patterns of both Emotional self and Intellectual self, do not view *yourself* as being bad or wrong. You know you have patterns; we all have patterns. But they're just patterns and you are far more than the sum of those patterns.

If you want some more insights about the two sides in you, here's a list of their possible reactions to help you out.

HONESTY QUESTIONNAIRE

Do any of the following patterns apply to you? If they do, put a tick mark or a circle next to them. Remember, if you own them in the first place you can work with them. 'Disown' them and they take shelter in the shadows of your personality. 'Me, pompous and arrogant? Never!' Watch out if you are saying '*No way* do I have that pattern' over and over again. Be especially mindful of ones you see in people around you, but never in yourself. Once again, bear in mind: that's one finger pointing out, but three fingers pointing back at you!

Patterns of Emotional self		Patterns of Intellectual Self	
Obstinate	Crying	Critical	Arrogant
Stubborn	Self-pity	Judgmental	Invalidates
Raging	Withdrawn	Acts like enemy	Represses feelings
Magical thinking	Addictive	Never compliments	Denies feelings
Timid	Rebellious	Never enough	Unrealistic
Drama queen	Head in clouds	Killjoy	Rationaliser
Whining	Manipulative	Argumentative	Intimidating
Defeatist	Complaining	Control freak	Pompous
Depressed	Cold	Self-righteous	Procrastinates
Irresponsible	Moody	Workaholic	Perfectionist
Whimpering	Violent	Withdraws	Defensive
Emotionless	Hysterical	Aloof	Disconnects
Zombie	Insatiable	Black and white thinking	Puts others down
Fearful	Self-centred		
Quitting	Resistant	Uptight	Elitist

Liar	Hopeless	Superior	Vindictive
Confused	Demanding	Constrained	Overanalytical
Defensive	Irritable	Narrow-minded	Acts stupid
Always tired	Impatient	Proper	Unappreciative
Phoney	Jealous	Rejecting	Nit picker
Victim	Resentful	Sarcastic	Doesn't listen
Martyr	Impulsive	Know-it-all	Serious
Self-absorbed	Self-destructive	Phoney holy	Not playful
Plays clown	Pouting	Discouraging	Self-centred
Love-buying	Seductive	Undermining	Manipulative
Dependent	Numbed out	Indirect	Blind
Grudge-carrier	Spoilt brat	Robotic	Cold
Self-conscious	Unreliable	Dogmatic	Tyrant
Hides out	Raging	Rigid	Driven
Obsessive	Overwhelmed	Compulsive	Overly precise
Impulsive	Has to win	Sloppy	Competitive
Pleaser		Prejudiced	Always has last word

How was that? Revealing? Painful? You might even be finding this procedure humorous. Remember, these are patterns, they are not the real you.

With an honesty cap on, can you see how you act with some of these behaviours in your life? Are you shocked? I know I was. In view of my tendency to 'have to be special' on the emotional side and 'arrogant' on the intellectual side, I was surprised I had any friends left at all. As for love relationships, the combination of being needy and seductive might work to attract someone. However, being very sarcastic and dead to my feelings would soon see them off. Being a rebel (emotions) and 'I know best' (intellect) might explain why my career path had got stalled. 'I was happier *not* knowing' was my childish re-action to this! There was quite a bit of work to do when I became more aware of how I operated.

As adults we may surprise ourselves by behaving childishly whenever we feel hurt, or threatened, or indeed if we want our own way about something. The childish Emotional self, rather than being all sweet and innocent, learns to be very manipulative. You only have to consider the politics in any organisation, to see lots of Emotional selves manipulating their way through life. Some do it through power games, others play 'poor little me, can you help?' while others rely on their physical or sexual charms. It's as if we're all desperately searching for ways to handle old pain, shame, guilt, humiliation and hidden anger. In an adult, our emotional history becomes a dangerous cocktail. We might even *know* that what we are saying or doing is ridiculous – and this of course leads us around a vicious cycle to yet more shame. We blurt something out in anger, cut someone out of our lives, and are then too ashamed to apologise or ask for help.

How do the Emotional self and Intellect interact?

Put the two together in the same person, and of course we get an inner conflict. Think of them as two people on opposite ends of a see-saw. At one end sits the Emotional self with its feelings, completely unable to take responsibility for its actions. At the other end sits the Intellect, thoroughly irritated by the Emotional self's irrational behaviour. The emotional side has strong mood swings, which go up and down, up and down. The intellectual side cannot keep the balance. Sometimes they are stuck and cannot move one way or the other. But that is not peace. It's paralysis.

The positive side of the Intellect wants to think clearly, while the positive side of the Emotional self wants to feel and express itself and to enjoy life. But do they manage that? Sadly not, because their negative sides are in control.

Emma's battle

A friend of mine, Emma, says that in the battle between the two she found the key to her weight problem. The chatter usually went like this:

Emotional self: 'I'm bored, let's go out and party.'
Intellect: 'No, there's work to be done.'
Emotional self: 'Well, I'm hungry. There are doughnuts in the kitchen.'
Intellect: 'You'll get fat, or should I say fatter.'
Emotional self: 'But we've done nothing but work all week. We need a little treat.'
Intellect: 'OK, just one.'
Two hours later: 'Look at you, you fat pig. How will anyone love you if you stuff your face all day?'

Sounding familiar?

Instead of working together to find true emotional intelligence, the two end up with a running fight. They can't decide on what to wear or spend money on. They make you wonder 'Am I in the right relationship?' 'Am I in the wrong job?' all the time. They're the maddening voices that shout or whisper all kinds of instructions, doubts, insults and messages of self-hate. They cause the endless chatter in your head that keeps you tossing and turning, and unable to go to sleep.

While these two are battling it out, we will repeat our self-destructive cycles of behaviour and end up fulfilling the negative prophecies. Our bodies will suffer with headaches, back pain and indigestion. After a few years, they might tell us they have had enough by developing chronic fatigue syndrome.

But the hardest part of all to bear is that we cannot hear

the wise voice of our Spiritual self. It is drowned out by the terrible racket these two make.

BRIDGING THE GAP: EXPRESSION OF THE TWO SELVES

Rather than having these big monsters shouting in my head all the time, now it's just these little shmos who occasionally drop round for tea.

ADAPTED FROM RAM DASS

You can learn to balance these two aspects through a variety of exercises and meditations, in which the Intellect and Emotional self get to meet and 'talk' to each other. Each one has the opportunity to express its gripes, grudges, frustrations, disappointments and anger. Through awareness followed by expression, the two find their own separate voices and realise that both aspects have an equal right to be heard.

Look at the issues you found for the Emotional self (see page 96), the Intellect (see page 97), and from the combined list (see page 99). What are the things that you would most like to see an end of? Be prepared to give voice to them by following the steps that one of my clients followed.

Looking for love in the wrong places

Brooke was working with us to resolve her co-dependent issues with men. Her child inside would desperately seek 'love' from the most unsuitable people. Her Intellect knew better, but was exhausted by working insane hours in a public relations company. She got up every day with a little voice inside saying, 'I feel miserable. Will someone, anyone make me feel better?'

I encouraged her to imagine herself as a childlike Emotional self and give voice to the emotional turmoil underneath. She cried out her fear and dreadful feelings of emptiness. Then, catching a wave of energy, she shouted out that her Intellect was meant to be taking better care of her emotions. 'You're meant to be grown up, aren't you? So help me out here. Teach me how to look after myself better.'

Next, I asked her to move a couple of feet and imagine she was standing in the position of her Intellect, which had just heard the Emotional self shouting. What would her Intellect want to say in response? She spoke loudly and clearly: 'Don't blame me for what you do! Stop acting so helpless. Tell me what your feelings are directly. Don't just hide them away all week.'

'Is that it?' I asked her when she was catching her breath. 'Or do you want to say some more'.

'More,' she replied.

'Don't let me down like this,' she continued. 'We can work it out. Why don't you, Emotional self, tell me when you're feeling down and we'll do something that you like to do.'

'Does the Emotional self have anything to say?' I asked.

'Yes, she does,' said Brooke. 'I'd like to get along better with you, my adult side. If you let me go out more, I won't sabotage your work efforts. I'll help you concentrate rather than space out and dream of Prince Charming.'

It seemed as if Brooke's Emotional self was preparing to make compromises and look for solutions. She checked in with her Intellect, who said it would also now consider things from the Emotional self's point of view. So the warring was over and it was time to let go and forgive what had happened in the past. They started to communicate with words of reconciliation, not anger or frustration. In this mood, I asked Brooke to draw up a truce between the two.

'Now that you've got the frustration out from both sides, listen to what each of them wants. Write down their demands and what they agree to.'

Brooke's childlike Emotional self wanted to leave work earlier and to go for trips on the weekend. She said it was also high time she learned how to rollerblade. Brooke's Intellectual self asked that her childlike aspect be willing to have regular meals and not to drink to excess on the weekends. The two parts agreed, and signed their names on the piece of paper. This contract or truce was then put on the fridge door, to remind Brooke every day of what had been agreed. I made her promise one more thing: if she broke the truce, she would forgive herself rather than punish herself all over again.

Brooke called me a few weeks later to say, 'I've stopped beating myself up since I realised that this war inside my head was an expression of two very different sides of me. Of course I still have the chatter, but I recognise it more quickly now. I tell them both either to shut up *or* let them have a good shout when I'm driving in my car. They each get a turn to let off steam at the top of their voices. As soon as I've done this, I get a feeling of real quiet which is absolutely wonderful. It's actually helped make my meditation practice much more powerful.'

The truce between these two aspects corresponds to 'Forgiveness' in the Awareness-Expression-Forgiveness-New Behaviour cycle of healing. When you find this truce, your higher nature can step through to play a far stronger role in your life. The next step is to find new ways of being and acting so that your change on the inside can be reflected on the outside.

CLEARING AND TRUCE

Have your own lists ready of the things you would most like to be rid of in your Emotional and Intellectual selves. Have another look at the combined list on pages 99–100 to add further fuel to the fire, if you need it.

Sort out the areas and situations roughly in order of how much charge you have around each. Which is the most highly charged? Is it the discussion about money with your partner? Is it to do with visiting the family you grew up with? *Imagine* yourself back in one of those situations. Make sure you separate what is an *emotional* reaction from what is *intellectual*. First feel yourself in the position of the Emotional self. Were you aware of not being true to your feelings at the time? Did you stop yourself from doing something that you had really wanted to do? Did you hurt someone when you really did not mean to? Give voice to what you are really feeling. Shout if necessary. Don't monitor yourself – just let go. When you have really let your Emotional self speak, then move on to the Intellect.

What was its response to the situation? What did it think, and how did it react? Again, listen to the voice inside, to any frustrations that might have been stored up, and let them out. Let this more adult side express itself 'unreasonably' for a change.

Have as many rounds as you need. Keep going until they have both said all they need to say and you can sense that there's no more charge left.

Next, have each of them talk to the other and ask their point of view. Make sure they really listen to the other side. When they have finished that, ask them if they are ready to move on from their old struggles. If they are, sit down and write a contract between the two. What can they both agree on? What new action might they take? Have them sign this truce.

FIRST AID

For a much quicker remedy, just as you are walking up to the podium or your boss's door, talk to yourself in an encouraging voice. Tell the scared part of you that this wiser part will look after you. Take three deep breaths, feel your feet on the floor, and say to yourself it's now, not the past. You have what it takes to do it. Become your own wise mentor.

SELF-WISH LISTS

Emotional self-wish list

Make a list of some of the things you know your emotional, childlike, life-loving aspect would enjoy. You might have been putting them off because you don't value your free time. It could be simple things, such as taking a walk or a cycle ride, going swimming or dancing, or taking a trip to a place you love. Next, decide a time to put these into action. If you still have doubtful thoughts or cynical reactions about doing things that bring you joy, write them down or speak them out loud. Tell your doubting or cynical Intellect that it's time to have some fun, and to let go of its control.

INTELLECTUAL SELF-WISH LIST

Now make a list of some of the things that you would love to learn, which would stimulate your mind. Consider things that in the past you might have felt you could not do, such as going to art galleries, or mastering computers, learning French cookery or a foreign language. When can you put these into action? If you feel your Emotional self resisting this, (for example, saying, 'I could never do that') you can tell it that you're not going to give up!

Once you have expressed the voices of your Emotions and Intellect, and discovered that they *can* listen to each other, you will find that the noise level in your own mind is much reduced. You can ask what the two aspects need and tune in to their positive suggestions. When the Emotional self feels it has a voice, it will be able to let you know much more about your full range of feelings. You will no longer live in fear of being undermined at crucial moments by old, conditioned reactions. When your Intellectual self feels in harmony with your Emotional self, it can do a far better job of sifting through all the information it comes across, both within itself and from the world outside.

Your body will in turn feel the benefit as it will not have to harbour so many tensions and conflicts. It can relax more, eat food for its health, not for emotional comfort, and sleep deeper. It can heal itself from your more self-destructive habits.

On top of all this, with greater peace of mind, you will find that your intuition, the voice that comes from within, grows stronger. Your Spiritual self is, simply, no longer drowned out and can give you clear guidance.

With this new found inner harmony, you are ready to begin exploring many new ways of feeling, thinking and being in the world. You are ready to step into a far richer range of responses. You are ready for a life full of change and possibility.

8
Living Life Fully Again

Become the change you want to see in the world.
MAHATMA GANDHI

Step Four: New Behaviour

Do you want to be able to live fully again? Do you long for a free life, not limited by fear, neediness or any of your old reactions? If you really want to change your life, know that you are opening a door through which may come all types of adventures and challenges. One of the biggest challenges is the fact that you will start to face *every* type of feeling. Life will be much fuller and richer as a result, and you will feel very alive. If you're ready for that, you are indeed ready for the fourth and final step of the process of change. You are prepared to step into 'New Behaviour'.

Our past experiences and heartbreaks have written our emotional history. By exploring our own emotions, we can change our ways and belief systems rather than repeating that history. We can consciously *learn* from the feelings we have within us to go forward on the path of change and self-discovery. Just as old anger can change to forgiveness, so old fear can turn to courage and shame to self-respect. We can turn our lives around by using our own emotions as the catalyst.

It takes an intense commitment to face the pain and the fear as well as the beauty and the joy within. When we are finally able to come to terms with blocked or unhealthy emotions, and to replace them with loving acceptance, the healing process will have worked deep within us. We will be able to love and accept love, the ultimate lesson of our lives.

The Emotional self has learned to listen and cooperate with our more adult and rational side. We know that the world is a safe place and that it is worthwhile expressing those emotions. We are committed to learning new ways of behaving. So what emotions lie waiting to emerge into a world full of the possibility of New Behaviour?

THE BIG FIVE EMOTIONS

We are all born with five main emotions: fear, anger, grief, joy and love. When expressed in a *healthy* way, fear protects us, anger allows us to set healthy boundaries, and grief enables us to shed healing tears over our losses. Joy provides the enthusiasm to live life with passion, while love provides the comfort of positive relationships. These make up our essential emotions, driving the myriad of feelings we may experience throughout the day.

However, these emotions can become blocked and unhealthy, and the one that suffers most is love. The word 'emotion' is derived from the Latin '*emovere*', meaning to move or emit motion. If we become e-motion-less, we stop moving, and our feelings stay stuck. It's easy to imagine how this might happen to a child. Not wanting to feel the pain of being left alone or feeling unloved, the small child defends itself by closing off some of its emotions. The layers become thicker as the years go on, until we find, in our adult years, that they have become almost impenetrable.

As Jung said, 'There is no birth of consciousness without pain.' When we start going back through those old layers, we may experience that original pain again. It's uncomfortable, but we have to do it to unblock our emotions. Having done that, then we can access our original joy and love.

We cannot go around these layers. We have to go through them. How much time do any of us spend getting in touch with our feelings? By examining these emotions in detail we can absorb the richness they contain to our lives.

Emotional beginnings: beyond indifference

We all go around denying how we feel about things because that's what we learn is normal. When we were young, it's likely that parents, schoolteachers and other adults said things like: 'No, of course you're not upset'; 'There's nothing to cry about' and 'You're fine. Be brave.' As children, we are constantly told that what we are feeling is not right – that it isn't 'really' what we are feeling. Our parents and teachers know best, so we believe them. 'You're right,' we tell ourselves. 'I don't really feel that.' Over the years, our emotional range gets smaller and smaller. We pack away our anger, our sadness and our vulnerability. Unfortunately, we also pack away our joy and our spontaneous wish to give and receive love.

The first step along the path to recovering our own emotions is to acknowledge a feeling. Whatever that feeling is. If you're angry, don't deny it because you have been told it's wrong to be angry. If you're upset or depressed, acknowledge that you are, don't reject the emotion. Of course, you may have to put off exploring it fully or expressing it until you're out of the office, but hold it there in your awareness.

Imagine that we have a huge source of love inside our hearts.

Unfortunately, rather than having that love overflow to all parts of our being and then to others, it becomes stuck. It can't come out. The layers of blocked emotions have backed up over time and love is buried under them.

There are five layers covering love. The 'cup of love' illustrates how these blocked emotions, like layers of hard-set concrete, prevent love from spreading in our lives. Each emotion is stacked up, reinforcing the barrier covering the love in our hearts.

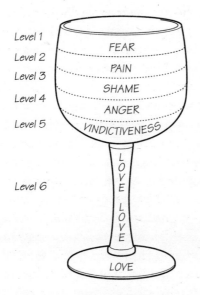

Level 1 — FEAR
Level 2 — PAIN
Level 3 — SHAME
Level 4 — ANGER
Level 5 — VINDICTIVENESS
Level 6 — LOVE LOVE LOVE

The Cup of Love

You need consciously to break through each of these levels. We will together explore each level in this 'cup of love', and in doing that find the way to new and healthy ways of behaving. Back in touch with each emotion, you will directly feel if there is unfinished business that must be dealt with. Once you have unblocked the old emotion, you can go further down, until you are back in the source of love that nourishes your life. Then your cup can indeed overflow to give love both to yourself and to others.

Level one: the natural emotion of fear

We come across fear very early on in our development. Fear is our 'survival' alarm bell and our physical protector. It is that instinctual 'fight or flight' we feel in the pit of our bellies when facing danger. It is also a channel to our intuitive sixth sense, which warns us that we could be in danger and creates ways for us to miss the plane that crashes or to step back onto the curb to avoid being hit by a car. Healthy fear subsides in time, and there is a feeling of gratitude and even an awe attached to it. *How the hell did I manage to escape that? Thank you God!'*

However, if as children we have experienced fear without a feeling of security around us, a blanket of fear and uncertainty may continue into our adult lives. In certain situations, we won't be able to respond to what is actually going on. We will be emotionally hijacked by an 'old brain' that stays in the past. We will 'react' rather than respond. We seem unable to get beyond the fear that gnaws away at us in the pits of our stomachs, and shows itself through such subconscious behaviour as panic attacks, free-floating anxiety, a fear of change, or perhaps a colourful array of phobias, for example the fear of spiders or heights. Distorted fear is an irrational frozen state of being. It makes us stammer in public, shrink into corners, hide away in our narrow mind-sets, and fail to take up any challenge. It also fills us with dread of what the future may bring, and so robs us of our spontaneity and joy in the present. We can be paralysed by it.

How to heal fear

There's nothing to fear except fear itself
Franklin D. Roosevelt

To heal our distorted reactions we need to take a walk back into the fears we experienced in the past, particularly as children. We need to overcome the fear of being who we really are and, in doing so, actively take back our power. Even though we have consciously decided to do this as fully grown adults, it remains a terrifying prospect. It still *feels* as if we are caught in the past as a little boy or little girl unable to defend ourselves. Part of us feels that we don't know what to do or where to run.

Awareness and expression of fear

By using visualisation techniques it is possible to re-visit childhood scenes and to release ourselves from the terror. The inner parent or imagined monster can no longer control or manipulate our reactions now. We can take back control of our lives.

Fear of confrontation

Isabel, an architect, was terrified of any sort of confrontation. Her company had initiated regular feedback sessions to encourage better communication among the employees. For her, these sessions were potential battlefields where she might be heavily criticised and even lose her job. The moment a comment was addressed to her, she felt criticised and, instead of responding in a normal way, she would clam up, start to sweat and retreat into her shell. Ultimately this made her very angry with herself.

I decided to use a technique called 'the elevator' with

Isabel. I wanted her to be able to see what was going on beneath her conscious mind. During this exercise, Isabel remembered being around the age of six and standing in front of her father's writing desk at home. He was telling her with a raised voice that she had been naughty that day and broken a lamp.

'But I didn't,' she tried saying.

'Don't answer back' her father shouted. His eyes were glaring at her and his face was blood red. As a child, tears of hopelessness had sprung to her eyes.

I encouraged her to reply to the father of her child-hood: 'What is it that you really wanted to say to him?'

'Please don't be so unfair. It wasn't me that broke the lamp.'

'Does he believe you?'

'No, he still looks angry.'

'OK then, you get his attention by raising your voice and being firm. Don't apologise.'

'That's hard for me.'

'I know,' I answered. 'Please do it anyway.'

'Don't blame me for something that I didn't do!' she bellowed. I was quite taken aback. Isabel the mouse had become Isabel the lioness.

'How did it feel to say that?' I asked her.

'Fantastic,' she replied. 'I feel that I have a voice after all.'

I led her back to her present age. 'Now imagine you're in a feedback session at work. Feel how different that might be now. Breathe into the feeling and let it be in all parts of you. Experience yourself as a powerful woman who can express herself in that scene. Let it become a model for future situations when there's feedback being offered.'

I checked in with Isabel over the next few months and

she told me that, along with going back through the elevator exercise again, somehow she had managed to change around her internal attitude. She was able not just to sit in a feedback session without panic, but also to contribute as an equal member of the team.

Try this exercise yourself if you want to explore a deeply held fear.

THE ELEVATOR

1. Imagine one of your fears. It could be a specific one, such as a fear of public speaking or a general one such as fear of success. See its effect on you and get in touch with how much you want to be rid of it.

2. Imagine an elevator in front of you marked 'Past Experiences'. Walk in and see the question *'How did I learn this fear?'* written on a control button. Push it. The elevator starts to go down. You go down at least seven levels through the years and through the levels of consciousness until the elevator stops. The doors open and you step out. The question still in your mind is *'How did I learn this fear?'*

3. First, get a sense of your age. Look at this scene in front of you. Who else is there? What is happening in the scene? Let whatever comes appear without judging it. If there is someone else there, what are they saying? How does it make you feel? Feel the effect on your body and breathing. Now imagine that you can talk to them and change your role in the scene. You can turn the scene around. Gone is the fear; instead you have power, confidence and a voice. Listen to yourself

as you 're-direct' the scene. If there is no one else there, talk to yourself in this new voice.

4. When you feel a shift inside, and have experienced an emotional turn, step back inside the elevator. Come back up to the present day. Now replay that shift inside imagining an actual, adult situation. See how good that feels? Write it down so you can better lodge it in your emotional and intellectual response. This can be your New Behaviour.

Level two: the natural emotion of pain

The cure for pain lies in the pain

RUMI

When we get past the paralysis of fear, then we can be in touch with and let go of our deeply held pain. This pain is a natural emotion, and is there for a reason. It's the grief for loved ones who have died, the sadness experienced for relationships that have not worked out, and the regret over lost opportunities in life.

The pain surrounding this grief could be very profound. We have always wanted to love and be loved, but instead we might have found coldness or rejection. So we protected ourselves with another wall between our tender love and the harsh world we lived in. This creates the thickest layer and the toughest one to crack. We believe it's just too risky to be vulnerable again.

Many of us are brought up to believe that tears are a sign of weakness, and that pain should be ignored or denied. If you don't show it, you are 'being brave'. *'She was so brave, she never shed a tear'* was a message I heard constantly as a child. Yet when we do deny our pain and grief it slowly begins to erode our natural zest for life. We end up deeply depressed. We become unaccountably guilt-ridden, remorseful, self-pitying or regretful. Often we escape from our pain by becoming 'aholics' of some kind: workaholics, foodaholics, dietaholics, exerciseaholics, adrenaline junkies, sex addicts and, of course, alcoholics. Our compulsive behaviour serves to block the pain from surfacing.

How to heal the pain

Being resigned to pain means you give up the connection with your spirit. We must translate pain into action and tears into growth.

Menachem Mendel Schneerson

Awareness: What do you do with the pain that lies over your heart? Think first about the messages you have received in life about expressing it. Have you been taught that grief is a natural part of your emotional make-up and that there are healthy ways of releasing it? If so, you are truly fortunate.

What old pain do you still feel the need to release? Meditate on what lies beneath the brave face you put on in society. Who are you protecting? Some of the themes might be very obvious to you. Others might be more hidden. What parts of your life do you still feel sad about? What parts of your life still make you feel vulnerable? Complete this sentence as quickly as you can, without filtering your response.

I still feel sad about . . .

Let the images come into your mind and remember them as snapshots in an album.

Then move on:

I still feel some pain about . . .

I still need to grieve . . .

I still need to let go of . . .

I miss . . .

Expression: Hopefully you have managed to get in touch with some old pain. When you feel that the time has come to release it, plan to go to a quiet place either in the house or in nature. With breathing and meditation, go softly into that painful space. Give it time and explore each of those 'snapshot moments' as deeply as you can. If tears come, let them come.

Tears allow us to express our pain and sadness in a natural way. In doing so, they clear our blocked emotions so we can begin to feel again. There are two types of tears: crying for help, and deep wracking sobs that involve the whole of the body. Crying for help often happens in a moment of extreme desperation and involves self-pity, fear and surface tears. However, it is the deep wracking sobs that enable us to completely let go of what we are holding in our hearts as well as in our bodies. They take us into a space so deep within ourselves that we may be afraid that we will never resurface again. Doing this, we are melting the layers over our hearts and connecting with our spirits.

This kind of crying does not have to last for long. The release that we feel in our bodies once the tears have subsided is often very profound. Once in a while, on our healing journey, however, we may reach a point when we think the tears will never stop. We find ourselves crying over the slightest thing and a voice inside tells us that we are being 'silly, over-emotional, or out of control'. However, rather than beating yourself up, think about it as giving your emotional self the opportunity – *and the right* – to finally release all those unshed tears. Letting go of pain and grief connects us not only with our emotional selves but also with our spiritual selves inside.

My brother killed himself a few years ago. He had been a bipolar or 'manic' depressive since a teenager, and felt that he would never climb up out of his sense of personal failure. His suicide was not a cry for attention; he simply threw himself under a London Tube train. He left behind a note that said, so sadly, 'I cannot feel love for myself or anyone else anymore.'

For much of my life, I have been cut off from my feelings

and unable to cry. Right after it happened, I took myself away from all the demands and the phone calls that come when a close family member dies. I had some old photos of him with me, a couple of letters and some other objects that brought back his memory. I sat in a quiet room. And then I cried as never before. Looking back, I know I couldn't have simply let go were it not that my heart had been shown how to grieve as an adult.

Do you have a place you can go to where you can honour your tender feelings? It does not have to be a whole room. It could just be a corner of one. There you can sit quietly, perhaps light a candle and 'stop your world'. We often feel too busy to stop. But we need to do just that to let go of our pain.

May releasing pain become a healing ritual for you.

Level three: the natural emotion of shame

If we are to get back to our original state of feeling loveable, we have to delve even deeper, beyond fear and pain, into our most profound emotions. We have to take a long walk into our own shadow of darkness. For many of us, the darkest place is one of shame.

It's healthy to feel remorse when you know you have consciously hurt someone or behaved in an inappropriate way. Or indeed, when you discover that you have unknowingly caused pain. When you know you have done something thoughtless or wrong, you are motivated to make amends and even grow from the experience. This is the healthy side of shame.

However, all of us carry around a sense of unhealthy shame. Shame is based on our emotional education. We learned it first when we were vulnerable children looking to have our views encouraged and reinforced by our parents, teachers and the society in which we grew up. Instead, what we found, in many cases, was criticism. We began to believe the criticism and, therefore, to feel that we ourselves were not good enough. Now we do anything we can to escape that horrible feeling; it makes us want to run away or to disappear behind our roles and our compulsive patterns. We become too ashamed to face or even show our shame, and instead put other people down to feel better about ourselves: *'There's nothing wrong with me – it's you who has the problem.'* It is a sad truth that many of those now in positions of power are driven deep down by unhealthy shame.

What does 'shame' mean to you? Embarrassment, guilt, going red in the face? Is it that overpowering feeling when you realise that you have said the most inappropriate thing? The moment you wish the floor would simply swallow you up? Is it the sense that you don't belong somewhere, but everyone else does? Are you ashamed of certain things that you have done, so ashamed that you find it hard to talk with anyone about them? Are you still carrying secrets around, letting them poison your insides with their accumulated power?

Shame lives at the extreme end of self-punishment. It is far stronger than guilt. Guilt says: 'I have done something wrong' while shame says: 'I am wrong'. It's not just the sense that I *made* a mistake. It's the feeling that I *am* a mistake. It's the voice that says: *'If people really saw who I was, they wouldn't want anything to do with me.'* Shame is that horrible sense of feeling that no matter what we do, how much money we make, how much therapy we have, we will still feel that there is something fundamentally wrong with us.

Naming your shame takes considerable courage because it means that you are laying yourself bare. It is not comfortable to feel that exposed. Yet, even though your shame may feel awful to you, to someone else listening to you with an open heart, it could be a mistake that helped you learn. The release that comes from finally freeing yourself is beyond words. You really need to release your shame, otherwise it becomes like a worrying dog constantly snapping at your ankles destroying your peace of mind.

How to heal shame

Awareness: What mistakes have you made in life that you feel really ashamed of? What are the secrets inside that you feel you could never let anyone know? Be gentle with yourself. If it does not feel safe to write them down, keep them in your mind. Is it the money you stole when you were a child? The affair that you had when you were already in a relationship? The business partner who you did out of their fair share? The abortion you had when you felt not ready to bring a child into the world? The times you have cut people out of your life? Look over your life, with this thought close to your heart: 'If I can forgive others, I can forgive myself.'

Expression: The most effective way to heal unhealthy shame is to express it by acknowledging it to someone you can truly trust. But if you do not wish to tell anyone, just write it down. You can learn to forgive yourself for these incidents of shame and to let go of the past. Do it ritually so that your consciousness is fully engaged in the moment. Give yourself the opportunity to unburden your soul from any of its shameful secrets, which have been keeping you chained to a life of inadequacy. Then you can enter into a healing space which is completely transformative.

It took years of emotional education to 'teach' you those deep feelings of shame, so re-educating yourself might also take time. If strong feelings come up, know that you're on the right path. You are counteracting the emotional education of your early years. If the feelings threaten to overwhelm you, ask for help. Know that many, many people feel the way that you do.

THE SCANNER

This first exercise is done individually. Get in touch with the feeling of shame inside you as well as, if appropriate, the actual shaming incident. Where does that shame live in your body? Use your hand like an X-ray scanner: pass it over your body, breathing gently. Is it in your head, your heart, your guts, your genitals? Take some deep breaths into that area. Breathe in light and breathe out the darkness. As you begin to relax, choose a message to affirm to yourself: 'I am good' or 'I am loveable' or 'I am OK just as I am.' Take the phrase that makes sense to you, something in which you can really believe. And yes, there still may be a part of you that rejects that phrase. Keep breathing in the light until that part is transformed.

THE BENEVOLENT WITNESS

Take a good friend, someone whom you can trust completely, to a quiet place where you will not be disturbed. Prepare them beforehand by saying that you have something important you wish to share with them. When you both feel comfortable, let them know what it is that has been troubling you. The first time is the hardest, but you will find again and again that you are accepted. You will probably find the trust levels deepen as you have given of yourself so generously. If it is not possible to find a friend, then make an appointment with a therapist, or find a group of like-minded people on a path of personal and spiritual development. Let the shame find words to break free from your heart.

RELEASING INTO FIRE

One wonderful ritual to release shame is based around fire. To give this even more power, first write down the things that have been eating away inside. Then, if the weather allows it, build a good fire and let it burn for a while until there are some embers glowing in the centre. Doing this outdoors is more powerful, as you then are open to a connection with the earth and the sky. Ask the fire to take away your shame: go up to it and tell it what you need to release.

Use a simple phrase such as: 'Fire, I release to you my sense of worthlessness,' or 'Fire, I give up to you my deep shame that I failed as a parent.' Stand there and see the flames burning away the years of torment that you have been giving yourself. Then take the page or pages you have written, roll them up, and put them into the very centre of the fire. See your shameful secrets literally burning away. Fire turns them into an energy that gives warmth and light to your spirit.

Letting go of shame allows you to feel in contact with your Spiritual self inside. You have gone through a thick level that says you're not good enough in order that you can come much closer to your original state – that of being good enough just as you are.

It's time now to move from the more tender emotions of fear, pain and shame, to the volatile, fiery ones of anger and vindictiveness.

Level four: the natural emotion of anger

The next layer covering love is anger. In its natural state, anger is a fiery passion that burns up old issues very quickly and effectively. Used healthily, it allows us to assert ourselves with firmness and clarity; to put our foot down by saying 'no!' and *meaning it*. It gives force to our voice and enables us to set acceptable boundaries within our relationships, especially when we feel other people are using us or are being disrespectful.

If we really feel trapped in our lives and long for change, anger provides us with the red hot courage to break out of the box: *'I can't stand this anymore. It has to change.'* The passion of anger spurs us on to greater heights and achievements. It fuels our basic conviction of what is right and wrong and gives us a feeling of dignity and pride in who we are.

Anger in its unhealthy state

Children are naturally spontaneous, and their anger is an instinctive expression that something is wrong with their world. Anger that is not healthily expressed during childhood turns into *historical anger* in our adult years. This historical anger can be automatically triggered by anyone who subconsciously reminds you of your childhood frustrations and feelings or rejection. Unless this is dealt with, it incites the vicious persecutor/victim dance which is a highly changeable and dangerous state. Either you become the persecutor, blaming and attacking others for what happens in your life, or you set yourself up subconsciously to become the 'poor me' victim of someone else's persecution. This can show up as physical or verbal violence, as unwarranted hatred towards a stranger such as a public figure, or entering into bitter vendettas. The 'neighbour from hell' syndrome is a good example. Historical anger creates wars, child abuse, gratuitous acts of violence, road rage, wife-battering, bitter hatred and so on – you can find its evidence in the newspapers every day.

However, many people stuff down their historical anger.

Repressed anger shows up not just as migraines, stiff shoulders and bad backs but also as heart irregularities, high blood pressure and stomach problems. One of the greatest distortions of historical anger is depression. We put energy into pressing down our old anger, and it ends up depressing our whole being. It is now estimated that over eighteen million Americans alone are suffering from some kind of depression, which is being treated by anti-depressant drugs. In the UK, between 7 and 12 percent of men will suffer from diagnosable depression in their lifetime. That figure is between 20 and 25 percent for women.

How to heal anger

Awareness: *Anger in the past*. Think back to your own childhood: what were the messages you received about anger? Perhaps it simply wasn't 'done' to show it, or it was a sign of weakness and you were shamed for feeling it – 'How *dare* you be angry?' Were you used as a scapegoat by one of your parents because of their pent-up rage? Maybe anger was never expressed in heated words, but your parents constantly jibed at each other. Their own repressed anger may have emerged in all kinds of ways. They may have dumped it through coldness, or sarcasm, through ignoring their children or by flinging guilt. Maybe that's what you learnt to do with anger.

There may have been actual physical abuse. Family violence is often a conspiratorial secret, kept firmly behind closed doors. It is this conspiracy which needs to be tackled if you are to find your own self-worth. Are you violent towards others or towards yourself?

If it helps, write what you can remember down on a piece of paper. Then start to think about how it has affected you as an adult.

You have to give yourself permission to break those unspoken family rules; to become angry with a righteous sense of indignation and take back your power. By letting it go, you can turn historical anger into an appropriate response, a natural emotion as it was always meant to be. It can become a valuable friend who stands up for your rights, not a loose cannon threatening to explode at any moment.

In the present. What anger are you carrying around now? Close your eyes and notice any reactions in your body. Perhaps your stomach is tensing up in fear at the thought, or you suddenly feel frustrated.

What happens now? How do you deal with your anger in personal relationships or in the work situation? Do you bite your anger back and are therefore constantly frustrated, or do you express it through sarcasm or some kind of revengeful behaviour? Just be truthful with yourself. Becoming aware that something needs to change in your life is the first step towards healing.

Expression: Anger needs *physical* movement to shift it. The best way to deal with anger is to go off somewhere you feel safe, and let it out somehow. Use your voice if you can. Sound is a very important aspect to ridding yourself of anger and hatred, so providing you aren't disturbing other people, let it out! Access the sound from the very depths of your belly. It's the noise your gut-felt anger needs to make in order to break free. If making a noise is a problem, you can shout deep into a pillow or utter a silent scream.

Anger is stored up in your body. Let your body be free of it through any expression that feels good to you – it could be through dance, painting, gardening, hitting a punch bag, kick-boxing, or even throwing out the clutter in your garage. You can run your feelings into the pavement, stamp on the floor, or swim with real thrashing strokes. Let go and trust in your own inner process. This is nature's way, even if we educated souls have forgotten it. You will know when you have had enough because you will feel cleansed and satisfied. It might be that afterwards you feel like crying or falling into a healing sleep.

Many people go through life practising a 'spiritual bypass', ignoring or burying their 'negative' feelings like anger and focusing only on love. Some are attracted to the spiritual life so they won't have to deal with the 'messier' emotions. But just ask someone living in a religious community if they feel love for their fellow residents all the time. No, they're just human like the rest of us. All of us need to look at and clear up the hard layers sitting on top of our own cup of love and, beyond our own, the universe's endless source of love.

Anger work is 'holy' work because by going through it you are brought closer to love for yourself and for others.

Level five: the natural emotion of vindictiveness

Don't get mad, get even.
Bumper sticker

Don't get even, get everything.
Advertising slogan for the film, *First Wives' Club*.

'Vindictiveness' is different to anger and lies deeper. It's a cold and calculating desire to cause hurt, to get back at those people who we feel have hurt us. It's not just a desire to exact revenge, it's an *addiction* to revenge. It drives that bitter and malicious behaviour which we *know* is going to do some damage. It's the voice that cruelly says, 'You owe me.' We carefully nurse an old grudge for years and years. With it in place, we will never forgive and move on.

Of course, we do not want to admit that we have this ugly side. We turn it around and become self-righteous. We tell ourselves: *'It's the principle that matters.'* We're subconsciously stating that being right counts for more than being happy: *'Even if it kills me, at least I'll go to my grave with my principles.'*

Whenever we hold on to an old grudge, we suffer. We drink this poison and slowly it begins to eat us up. There's even a perfectly legal way of getting our vindictive wishes fulfilled. It's called taking someone to court. If we win, for a while we feel satisfied. But what real ongoing satisfaction does that win give us on a spiritual level?

One way to see our own sense of vindictiveness is to examine our role as victim. These days it is often said that the victim has the most power. You will get more sympathy being a victim, and that is what the Emotional self, stuck in childhood, needs. If we get sympathy, once again someone is taking care of us.

How to heal vindictiveness

Awareness: Who are you aware of needing to get back at? Who do you feel has done you wrong? You feel that it wouldn't work just to get angry at them. You want to punish them and to *know* that they have suffered. At different times in our lives, we are all capable of harbouring this feeling. Be honest with yourself.

Expression: Remember that the idea of someone in your mind is the 'reality' you carry around. It's up to you whether you perceive them as an object of fear and hate or not. If *they* are not going to change, and *you* need peace of mind, you are going to have to do something to change your mind's image of them.

THE WIPE-OUT

If you have a particular sense of being hurt or used – for example, being raped, or sexually or physically abused, what you might need to do is a 'wipe-out'. Here you imagine your perpetrator in front of you and, using a pillow or similar object, you act out your wish for revenge. You imagine 'wiping them out' so that you are not terrified of them in future, or held in their power forever.

Remember, as you visualise this person, that you are dealing with their dark side, the aspect of them that has hurt you. This is not really their physical self, nor is it their spiritual self. Imagine putting them down on a cushion in front of you. Rather than just telling them what they have done to you, start indulging your fantasies of what you at some point would like to have done to them. Remember that you are defending yourself. If it gets ugly, let it get ugly. It's a poison that needs to come out. You might imagine strangling them, drowning them, running them through with a sword. Do what you need to do to take your power back first, physically. Give your mind a chance to overcome the feeling of powerlessness.

When you express yourself in this way, breathe and feel the energy running through you. Feel this as your own natural power. Put your hand on that part of the body where you feel this power most strongly. Anchor the feeling of strength right there. If you feel vindictive or powerless again, put your hand on that point and you will be reminded of your innate power instead.

THE CLEANSING VOICE

We often have very strong feelings, towards ex-boyfriends and girlfriends, or former husbands and wives. It seems that those we have at one time most loved are the ones we find it easiest to hate. They have hurt us so much, caused our love to feel blocked, and now our Emotional selves want to see them punished.

To express the old poison you might have in you towards those you have loved, first imagine them in front of you. This time, though, you are not hitting them, but claiming your power back through your voice. They may not be in your life anymore physically but they exist strongly in your mind. With sounds from your gut, let them hear your rage, your frustration, your wish to be understood, and – if it's true – your wish that they suffer. When you feel 'spent', sit down and breathe.

As you breathe, feel your energy and strength. With one hand, anchor that place of power in your body. You have the power to learn lessons from that relationship and move on.

Beyond expression to forgiveness

Once you have expressed your vindictiveness, you can move on to the next stage, forgiveness. Remember, just as with your parents, you do not have to condone their *behaviour*. They may truly have acted in cruel and stupid ways. They are guilty for what they did, just as we are guilty for our mistakes, and still we can move on in life rather than being possessed by the past.

To forgive them, know that they also have a precious soul, a spiritual side beyond their personality. Imagine that you are back in your mind's sanctuary, where you feel calm and at peace. There visualise in front of you the Spiritual self of the person you have been shouting at, or completed the 'wipe-out' with. Walk up to them and look them in the eye. Look deep into their eyes to see their pure essence. This part has never wanted to hurt you. They may even have come into your life for you to learn something.

If you still feel that the person has some power over you, try imagining them much younger than they are now, as if they were once again a child. Go to your mind's sanctuary and picture yourself sitting down with them. Have a conversation to heal any past misunderstandings. Ask them how they learned to act the way they did. Listen to what they tell you and let it in. Take what you learn so that you can heal the dark feelings inside of you.

Forgiveness might not occur on the first time you do this. It might take a few tries. You might have to do it every day for a week or a month. Keep at it for your own healing and wish to change. Through it you will find the most satisfying New Behaviour, to truly love yourself and others.

Level six: the strongest and deepest emotion is Love

Love is the most powerful and still the most unknown energy of the world.

Pierre Teilhard de Chardin

Love, they say, conquers all. Love is the great healer. Love is the universal emotion. We are fascinated by it, yearn for it, live and die by it, sing about it, fight wars over it. Yet it's hard to describe love. Even though most of us 'know' what it is, we cannot say what it is.

Love is the connection between our human and our spiritual sides. It reminds us that we are spiritual beings having a human experience. It's the thread running through our lives, from the moment of conception to the moment of death and in the hereafter.

Love is a lesson we may have once learned, but have forgotten. We need to find a way to stay connected to it.

Most of us do not live permanently in a state of love or loving. If asked, we would probably say that our strongest experience of it is when we 'fall' in love. But falling implies that we lose our sense of balance. When we fall in love we are treated to a marvellous cocktail of chemicals making us feel fully alive. But often, the chemicals do not last long. We may carry on awhile in the relationship until we decide one of us is no longer 'in love'. Falling in and out of love, though, is not healthy love. What is?

This is the Hoffman Process definition of Love:

Love is the Flowing, the Outpouring, the Rendering of Emotional Goodness to Yourself First – and then to Others in Your Life.

Awareness: How easy is it for you to *say* that you love yourself? How easy is it for you to *feel* love for yourself? What indeed does 'love' mean to you personally? Most of us have such a charge with it that the very phrase, 'I love you' carries enormous emotional and psychological weight. An inner conversation is held. For example: 'He says he loves me. Is he serious? Does that mean he's ready to commit?' Or the other version, 'She just told me she loves me. Does that mean she's going to get all serious now? Wait a minute, I think we're rushing things a bit here.' Its power can also become reduced through over use; for example, when we end each phone call by quickly saying, 'Love you.'

How was the phrase 'I love you' used in your family? Some people grew up never hearing it, and therefore as adults it exists beyond their known world. They dismiss the phrase as something from a Hollywood movie. Some of us grew up hearing it often, but always with conditions attached 'I love you, so please would you do this for me?' or 'I love you. Please don't ever leave me.'

Expression: If you are aware of any negative patterns and beliefs around 'love', you will need to disconnect emotionally from them. You can build a healthy barrier between you and the patterns or beliefs by writing them down or using your voice. Do this until the old reaction inside of you has gone.

To express love in a healthy way, there are at least two more things that you could do. One is to think *who* you have been putting off telling that you love and then go and let them know. The other is to think what might you do for *yourself* as an act of self-love. After all, if you wanted to form a loving bond with someone, you would 'romance' them, perhaps by inviting them out on a date, or taking a special trip together. Treat yourself to a proper date! If there really was only one thing you could change in your life, make it this: change the pattern of 'I'm not good enough' to the healthy one of 'I am loveable just as I am.'

The great healing power of love is very simple. Once you are connected to healthy love, you will not spend your life looking to fill a void in your heart. You will not be chasing the promise of a relationship out of need. You will have that love relationship with you at all times. Because of it, you will find people around you being attracted by and responding to your over-flowing cup of love. You will also be able to connect with the order of love in the universe. You might find this in nature, through music or art, or in your spiritual tradition. It is every-where, and it is limitless.

By working down through the levels of your own Cup of Love, you have faced all your old emotions and given yourself the chance to respond to life with the full range of natural emotions. You are now able to draw on a feeling of abundant love. With all that is available to you, you can create wonderful new ways of being both with yourself and with others.

You have given yourself the most wonderful gift – that of living fully in the present, nourished by love.

PART TWO

CHANGING YOUR LIFE

In the first section of this book, you were led through the basic steps of the Hoffman Process. You looked at your own patterns of behaviour and belief systems inherited from the past. You contacted your own spiritual values and defined your vision of how you wanted to live your life. You came to an under-standing and forgiveness of the past so that you could live in the present. You were then taught how to balance the emotions and the intellect to gain peace of mind. You worked through all the old emotions to return to a state of love.

Having done this work, you are in a wonderful position to apply the steps and change every aspect of your life for the better. Have you ever had a really good clear-out in your house and thrown out all the excess clutter? Remember the feeling? You no doubt felt satisfied and renewed with fresh energy. You would probably have been excited about the prospects for your life in general. With this extra energy, you decide to head out of the front door and into the world to see what else you can clear up.

You now have that energy and that motivation to continue your own process of change.

9
Transforming Your Approach to Love

Life is either a great adventure, or nothing.
HELEN KELLER

For many of us, the first thing in our lives we would look at changing would be our relationships, especially the closest ones where love is involved. It's through these that we are reminded of the connection with our own hearts.

If we share our lives with someone, they can very easily provide a mirror for us to see our own behaviour. In interacting with them every day we see our own potential to love, to argue, to be intimate and to reject. In short, with a loved one, we will see our own best and worst behaviour. We will be confronted with the choice between love and indifference, between facing ourselves or avoiding the issues that stand in our way to personal fulfilment. If we find it hard to find or to stay in a relationship, then we need to look at what is getting in the way. Let's take a good look at the reality of relationships and find ways of making healthy changes.

Imagine: you've just walked into a party, and there's someone standing in front of you. You are instantly attracted to them. Even more than that, you seem to 'know' what they are thinking and feeling. You look at the expression in their eyes and feel that they understand you, too. You start talking and, wonder of wonders, the two of you have many things in common. Pleasantly flushed with excitement, you promise to call each other. Before you leave, you feel that you have known them for ages. Oh my goodness, you think, perhaps this is The One, My True Love!

Maybe it is, but this could all be a pleasant fantasy in your mind, one that will not end like a fairy tale. What is going on inside your head at this point?

Perhaps you know this scenario very well from your own personal life. You are attracted time and again to prospective partners who you feel will be able to provide you with the love that you crave. After a brief infatuation stage, you feel disappointed and sooner or later you leave or get dumped. How come, you ask yourself, there are so many undeserving people in the world?

The fantasy of Mr or Miss Right appearing is the hope in our childlike Emotional selves that a perfect, unconditionally loving 'parent' will appear and take care of us. We live in hope of finding once again that love that we so wanted and needed as a child. Since our own parents could not meet our expectations, we are setting ourselves up for disappointment and bitterness. We suffer and our partners suffer more from the shadow of the past than what actually is in the present.

We are all carrying something into our present lives that should have been left in the past. We *transfer* or carry over old memories and images on to people we meet in our everyday lives.

If we have unresolved relationships with our parents and the significant other carers in our lives, those issues will come to haunt us until we have learned the lesson we were meant to learn, and then healed the past. It's not surprising that – especially in love relationships – those left-over issues with our parents and carers can surface. Here we find that the old stories about being loved or rejected, needing or being needed, are played out every day. It's therefore in love relationships that we stand to win or lose the most by letting go of the old baggage.

In order to keep any love relationship in good health, we need to be able to go beyond negative messages about love and intimacy. We need to make sure that we have cleaned up any carry-over from the past, what psychologists refer to as 'transference'.

So what might be standing in the way of your relationships today?

Awareness: mum and dad might still be around!

In the same way that we recognised our parents in our behavioural patterns and roles, so we might see their influence in our love relationships. Stanley Stefancic, one of the earliest Hoffman Process teachers, composed a simple ditty that summed this up all too well:

> *Wherever I go, whoever I see,*
> *I see Mummy and Daddy,*
> *And they see me.*

Yes, everywhere a part of our mind, the old emotional brain, 'sees' our internalised parents. We transfer those images of our childhood mother and father with whom we grew up and shared our deepest emotional experiences not only onto our lovers, but also to a lesser extent onto our friends and work colleagues, especially, our bosses (see Chapter Ten). The strongest reactions occur in an adult love relationship where, instead of seeing a normal, healthy love and need for each other, the spectre or ghost of the childhood relationship may be raised. If the story of childhood was one of physical or emotional absence, then that story will be replayed like a tape on a continual loop until we either get fed up to the point of breaking it, or being broken by it. It's no wonder the divorce statistics are so high.

Look for times in your relationship when you have felt ignored, irritated, cut off, needy, wanting approval or very critical. Next, check if these reactions have been happening on a regular basis. Sure, your partner may have something to do with it – it does take two to tango – but the objective is to take self-responsibility. You are clearing up your story. If they do the same with theirs, all the better.

LEAVING THE PAST BEHIND: FINDING BALANCE IN THE QUADRINITY

By learning to recognise these carry-overs from the past you can prevent any self-sabotage and respond to the actual *people* you meet. You can learn to respond rather than being emotionally hijacked by old patterns of behaviour. If it's at the start of a relationship, remember to catch yourself before lighting the explosive fuse. Marianne Williamson put it very aptly in her book *Return to Love*: 'The problem is not that you met him, the problem is that you gave him your phone number.'

You can teach the rational part of your mind, the Intellect, to be aware as well as warn of possible danger in a relationship. Your Intellect can protect potential disasters by recognising unsuitable partners, for example! Meanwhile you will have to acknowledge your Emotional self for its response, especially if the response is one that takes you out of your power. If you feel overly needy with someone, or hurt or angry, imagine that you are speaking with compassion to a vulnerable child inside you, and say firmly but lovingly, 'No, you and I do not need to go there again.' Saying 'no' to old patterns, and meaning it, is itself a powerful move towards self-healing and integration. The next move is to recognise that there is enough love already within you, once you move down through the various levels of emotion (see Chapter Eight).

Meanwhile, another strong inner voice of direction can come from your Spiritual self. Stay in touch with your vision of what you want in a relationship (see page 39). See how you want to share your life with this person and how easy it is to be with them. Vision the joy, laughter and creativity you can enjoy together. Your Spiritual self is the part of your Quadrinity most connected to your eternal truth. In moments of silence, drop into its pool of wisdom and you will be guided to choices based on love, not fear.

These voices inside of Intellect, Emotions and Spiritual selves make up the three non-physical aspects of your Quadrinity. Remember to check in with the aspects again and again until it feels completely natural, like getting up in the morning. These three are learning to work together as a supportive team with your best interests at heart because of the work you completed in the first half of this book. Of course it's challenging to break such deeply ingrained relationship patterns, but you need to break out of them to build healthy relationships.

ATTRACTION/REPULSION: WHAT'S REALLY HAPPENING?

It's worth examining our strongest and instant reactions to people to see the link with the past. Throughout life, we get especially caught up in two. They can simply be called 'love' and 'hate'.

Is it 'true' love?

Who are we most likely to fall in love with? A well-known relationship expert, Harville Hendrix, claims that we are attracted to the people who most closely match our parents in order that our childhood love wounds can be healed. In *Getting the Love You Want*, Hendrix writes:

> Love we are seeking has to come not just from another person within the context of a safe, intimate relationship, but from an 'imago match' – someone so similar to our parents that our unconscious mind has them fused. This appears to be the only way to erase the pains of childhood. We may enjoy the hugs and attentions of other people, but the effects are transitory. It's like the difference between sugar and Nutrasweet. Our taste buds may be deceived by the taste of artificial sweeteners, but our bodies derive no nourishment from them. In just the same way, we hunger for love from our original caretakers or from people who are so similar to them that on an unconscious level we have them merged.

In this old, emotional part of our brain – the Emotional self – we still want to be taken care of by our parents. We want to be loved unconditionally by them. We are instinctively attracted to those people who possess the same kind of behaviour patterns as our parents. Of course, it also helps if they are physically similar. This attraction is strong, like a flame to a moth, and we may get severely burnt in the run of events because we end up playing out some kind of child role with them.

Do you remember the first time you met your current or recent partner? What was it about them that you found so attractive? As you got to know them better, did they fulfil the expectations that you had of them? *Could* they ever fill the high expectation you might have had?

'I know I won't like them'

On the other hand, we have all had the experience of meeting someone and instantly disliking them – for perhaps the way they look, or carry themselves, or their tone of voice. We do not know it consciously, but what is happening is very probably again a strong unconscious reminder of one of our parents. It could also be a figure of authority whose approval we needed, like a teacher at school. Instead of being attracted, however, this time when our old love wound is re-triggered we do not attempt to heal it. We defend ourselves against it.

This reaction can strike at any time and anywhere. You meet someone and see them as arrogant, bossy, ignoring you, humiliating you, not giving you the time of day. It's hard to admit, and indeed it may be buried far beneath our pride, but the truth is often that we yearn to be *acknowledged* and liked by them. Not wanting to be hurt again, we 'decide' to dislike them or even hate them – and wonder why our friends find them perfectly reasonable people.

These shadows from the past mean that we can prejudge many people. That pre-judgement or prejudice might even apply to every member of one gender. A simple fact that could strike 50 percent of humanity from a list of possible friends!

Carrying around the past in this way, we lose our own sense of personal power. We compulsively invest time and energy in demanding something from people that is not theirs to give. Though they may love us, they can *never* replace the mother or father of our childhood. To get beyond this, we need to delve into our past to heal the old hurt and feelings of left-over rejection. Having done the work on your parents in the first half of this book, you are in a great position to change your old ways. You also know the wisdom of tapping into the endless source of love in your own cup of love.

It is firstly up to *us* to change, however much we would love our partner, friend or lover to change *their* patterns. They are who they are just as we are who we are. Once we accept them the way they are, and understand the problem is mainly caused by our *perception* of them, our relationships can change. We are taking responsibility for our role, not forcing change on someone else. People only change if and when they want to. But if your partner likes the change they see in *you*, then they might be more motivated to change themselves.

'It's your fault': war between the sexes

A bright and attractive couple in their thirties, Eleanor and Barry came to see me when they felt their relationship was headed for the rocks. There was still some love between them, but more and more it was getting buried beneath a lack of respect that was wearing them both down. To get some more insights into how they operated, I asked both what bugged them about the other person.

When they started to share their irritations, the situation did not look pretty. Eleanor complained in a whining voice that she was never allowed to give her point of view. Barry screamed back: 'But I'm always telling you that you have a voice in this relationship. Don't give up so easily!' I pointed out that this last comment could be perceived as critical.

Eleanor told Barry, 'You're always telling me what to do and how to do it.' I reminded her that we were aiming towards more self-responsibility at this point.

'How can *I* take responsibility for *her* behaving like a doormat?' asked Barry, glaring.

'And *I'm* not taking responsibility for *you* being such an arsehole,' replied Eleanor. It was fast deteriorating into a scene from a 'Jerry Springer' show.

I said we would have to take some time out and gave each of them a task. Eleanor had to write down if there were any similarities between what Barry did and what her mother and father might have done when she was a child. In the same way, Barry had to think if Eleanor was reminding him of what either his Mum or Dad did. When they had finished, I asked them to read out from their lists and agree not to interrupt the other.

Eleanor went first. It turned out that she had a very dominant and critical father. The family household was ruled by the code: 'My way or the highway'. In her mind both her father and Barry told her what to do rather than asking her what she might want to do.

On his side, Barry had a mother who was an expert in playing victim. According to her, the world was a cruel place and her husband, Barry's father, was someone to be feared. There was no point in speaking her mind. She had never learned to drive and was frightened of public transport, so whether by choice or circumstance she became dependent on her husband to show her the world beyond the house. She had no say in the family finances and so Barry was raised believing that a man would be in total command of the money side of things.

The combination of Eleanor's father and Barry's mother 'living in their house' seemed designed for misery. Seeing how she carried memories of her father allowed Eleanor to understand her perceptions of Barry in a more forgiving way. She promised to listen more carefully. Barry meanwhile saw his need to remove the label of 'victim' that he had assigned Eleanor in the early days. He let her know that he would give her an equal say in their decisions.

It has not been easy for Barry and Eleanor, but it has

been worth it. Too many relationships end up in actual or virtual divorce because we don't want to work through our issues. The easier way is simply to say that it's all the other person's fault and trade them in for another model. 'Now this one I feel really understands me and knows me', we tell ourselves if we catch a new one. Only thing is, if we do not deal with what's left over, the cycle is going to happen all over again.

HOW TO CHANGE: AWARENESS, EXPRESSION AND FORGIVENESS

The first step out of the messy games that are played is to become *aware* of your habitual reactions. By acknowledging an old reaction you can start to break the energy held by that pattern. What's more, you bring yourself back into the present rather than staying locked in the old situation. You start to distinguish between what's actually happening and your *perception* of what's happening. The following exercise allows you to see with far clearer eyes what lies between you and the reality of a present-day relationship.

RELATIONSHIP CHECK-UP

1. Think about some of the things concerning your partner or loved one that really get you annoyed. If you are not currently in a relationship, think about the last one that you had. Have you ever found a partner to be over-critical, nagging, distant, or closed down? Are there times when you feel ignored by them, not listened to,

discounted or worthless? Are they on occasion bossy, dominating, manipulative or stubborn? Is it when they play hopeless, or martyr or victim that gets you all fired up? When do you have the strongest emotional reactions to them? What is it that they are doing at the time?

2. Make a written list of the three strongest negative reactions you have had to your partner or loved one. Put down the actual event – was it discussing the money situation, where to go on holiday, how to bring up the kids, whose turn it was to clean up? Next, write down what the feelings were that you had in that situation – it might have been anger, hurt, fear or frustration.

3. Now get in touch with your own reaction to them at the time. What was the underlying pattern? Was it one of distrust, needing their approval, withdrawing, giving up, or resignation ('what's the point?'). Was it one where you felt a need to go on the attack, where the pattern might have been 'aggressive' or 'dominating'?

4. Would you consider the possibility that there are some old images and memories in your head that are colouring your reactions to others? Looking back, do you remember your father as being critical or shut-down? Was your mother nagging or controlling? Which one of them might have been manipulative or stubborn at times? Did your mother or father, or significant surrogate, play victim or martyr? Remember, that you are not starting the cycle of blame but are taking responsibility for your own handed-down baggage.

5. You may now be in touch with a feeling and the reaction you had. You have also identified perhaps which parent or surrogate a partner could have reminded you

of. Being honest, is it possible that your reaction in the present day was stronger than this person deserved? Have you brought your own issues of the past into the present situation?

Taking responsibility means that we own our perceptions for ourselves rather than making rigid statements about what we deem to be right or wrong. We stop blaming others for not being how we think they 'should' or 'ought' to be. Rigid opinions cause conflict, whereas seeing something as our point of view shows a willingness to explore a situation and find a settlement.

Gerald Jampolsky, who wrote the bestseller *Love is Letting Go of Fear* explains how we can best return to loving each other:

Most of us manifest a condition which could be called 'tunnel vision'. We do not see people as a whole. We see just a fragment of a person and our mind often interprets what we see as a fault. Most of us were brought up in a home and school environment where emphasis was placed on constructive criticism, which is usually a disguise for finding fault. To experience unconditional love, we must get rid of the evaluator part of ourselves. In place of the evaluator, we need to hear our strong inner voice saying to ourselves and others: 'I totally love and accept you as you are.'

On the road to peace: Expression

If the first step to loving someone just as they are is to acknowledge our old critical voice, the next step is to *express* it safely so we can let it go.

This is a very bold step. But if you are dedicated to growing in your relationship, then take that step by letting your partner know what you have been carrying around. It's the same principle as with shame (see Chapter Eight): by sharing it with a benevolent witness, you can find a tremendous relief.

Follow the steps of the 'relationship communication' exercise below. Make sure before you begin that the main thrust of the emotional reaction is gone. Check in quickly both with your Emotional self and also with your body, which might be holding tension. If you still feel angry or upset with your partner, he or she may immediately become defensive and so not able to listen to you. Agree on a time and place where you won't be disturbed. Make sure that for both of you, the intention is to clear, not to dump, and that you'll be using 'I' statements. Remember that you will be looking at your *own* perceptions and patterns.

RELATIONSHIP COMMUNICATION

This exercise has five parts:
1. Identifying who your partner was in your eyes – which parent or carer.
2. Naming the situation – be specific, not 'you always do such and such'.
3. Putting a name to the feeling – anger, sadness, not 'I felt you were being a real pain'.
4. Calling the pattern – 'abandoned', 'ignored' or 'victim', for example.
5. Appreciating the other person once you are finished.

If you feel that both of you understand the intention of this exercise (clearing, not dumping) then take these steps with your partner. You may feel the need to 'buy an insurance policy' first or minimise it by saying that it was really nothing big, or that they're just the most wonderful person and it's you who's wrong. Stop those old patterns! Be authentic to the feelings and reactions you had at the time so that you can acknowledge them, express them, and work them through. When you then go on to appreciate your partner, you are doing what corresponds to *forgiveness* work. You are sending a signal that you can leave the negative charge behind, and that the slate has been wiped clean of that incident. By being in honest communication, you are showing yourself and your partner that you can change. You are demonstrating a 'New Behaviour' and, in so doing, opening the doors to whole new possibilities for your relationship.

Healthy New Behaviour

Wanting to clear up some unfinished business, a lawyer called Josh sat down one day with his wife Martina, pen and paper in hand, to look at some of the emotionally charged issues that remained between them. They chose a time when the kids were asleep and there was no pressure of work to interrupt them. The phone was put on to answering machine mode.

First, they made a list of situations in the past few weeks where they had felt a strong reaction to each other. For Josh, one time was in the company of Martina's actor friends when he had felt ignored and out of place. Another time was when he felt Martina was making huge demands upon him by repeating how much she wanted to spend time with him. The third was when they were packing everything for a trip with the kids and he felt bossed around.

Martina's list was made up of the times when she had

felt Josh was lecturing her about the environmental impact of using the car, when she felt he was not interested in her, and when she thought that he was avoiding spending time with their children.

They then put their pens down and each took a deep breath. They had been together for nearly ten years, and had known each other for over twenty, but they knew there were still lots of learning opportunities in their relationship. They agreed that Martina would go first.

'Josh, I transferred my father on to you when I felt you were lecturing me about cleaning up the environment. I felt very small and stupid, and the pattern I went into was to shut down.'

'Thank you,' Josh replied. They each took another deep breath. Now it was Josh's turn.

'Martina, I transferred my father on to you the other night when we went out to dinner with your friends. I felt awkward and the patterns I went into were "shy" and "no one's interested in me".'

'Thank you,' she said. Another deep breath, and their heartbeats were approaching normal again.

'Josh, I transferred my mother on to you after dinner last night when you said you had to go back and do some work in your office. I felt unimportant and worthless. The patterns I went into were "blaming" and "playing victim".'

'Thank you.' They left it some time before it was Josh's turn again.

'Martina, I transferred my mother on to you when you said, "Don't you want to spend some time with me?" last night after dinner. I felt frustrated and the patterns I went into were "feeling guilty" and "feeling manipulated".'

During this communication, what had been unspoken and potentially charged with emotion had come out into the open. Once it had been expressed, it could no longer hold the same power over them either as a brooding resentment or a poisonous sense of defeat. On top of that, by exposing their own vulnerability – the vulnerability of their Emotional selves feeling awkward or rejected, small or stupid – they were letting the other know that they were more interested in peace than power. They were laying down their arms in order to find a truce.

When you are in close contact like this, both physically looking at each other and verbally communicating, you will be able to sense each other's reactions and feelings. We can spend so much time organising our own busy lives that we forget to make a priority of time together with our partners, and so neglect to tune into each other. Connecting like this builds a wonderful bridge and reminds us of the love we all have to give. Remember to keep eye contact while you are talking. You will have a far deeper sense of compassion seeing the real being through eyes which Shakespeare called 'windows of the soul'.

Martina and Joss had each gone twice, and agreed that that was enough for now. They checked that they had no remaining charge about those incidents before talking about what they appreciated in each other. Looking at each other fondly, Josh appreciated Martina for the thoughtful gifts she brought him back from a shopping trip. She appreciated Josh for truly listening to her. Having delved through the layers of old emotions, they were now far more connected to their own 'cup of love'. With the old reactions out of the way, they could be in contact with their own Spiritual self, which comes from a place of unconditional love. In the same way, we know that our love has a spiritual basis. We may not love all the patterns our partner has, but we can love the wonderful Being that is them, beyond those patterns!

You can follow these same simple steps to building and keeping a healthy relationship. Be *aware* of what comes up for you day by day both within yourself and with your partner. If what has come up involves that partner, your awareness needs to be followed by an *expression* of what you have done or said to your partner that has had a bearing on your relationship. Hopefully you will have established a trusting atmosphere whereby the mistakes of the past can be forgiven. *Forgive* your partner if the mistake has been theirs, in person if it feels appropriate, or within yourself if not. Ask for forgiveness if you have been at fault and if by asking you do not harm the relationship. Forgiving and being forgiven, you can then move on to another day and another level in your relationship. You can leave the past behind and find 'new ways of behaving'.

You have seen how the four steps of the process of change can be applied in a direct way to benefit your own life. In love relationships we have an enormous amount to gain by changing our old ways of being and relating, which is one of the main aims of the process. But this process asks for something more – that you share this universal gift of love, and not just keep it to yourself. You will find in these relationships that what you have learned about giving and receiving love will be put to the test. The test is worth it, for it is mainly through love relationships that we discover that we are in essence loving beings.

10

Enriching Your Relationships with Friends and Colleagues

Friendship is a single soul dwelling in two bodies.

ARISTOTLE

As we've seen, patterns left over from the past can have an enormous impact on our relationships in the present. It may well be true that we have most to win or lose in the high-risk, high-reward world of love relationships, but our social environment is largely made up by friends and colleagues at work. That being the case, it's worth looking at how we can make even more of our relationships in those areas. We'll be focusing on what makes for healthy friendships, how to repair ones that have gone off-track, how to build good boundaries, and how to develop practices that maintain these relationships in a good state.

Do you feel that there is room for you to have more trust in people, not to mention more fun and shared learning experiences? Do you feel that you can communicate your feelings and sense of truth with other people, or do you hold yourself back for fear that your words might hurt someone or be used against you? Are you content with the variety and richness of your friendships?

The process of change makes us not only *aware* of what we habitually do, but also encourages us to *take responsibility* for what we do. Once we have acknowledged our part, we can find new ways of acting, especially in the way we communicate. It's so tempting to want to change the other person, but of course, there's only one person we can guarantee changing and that is ourselves. The good news is that we do not risk being hurt as much here as in our love relationships, but we can *still* learn a great deal more about recognising and sharing our sense of reality. This chapter will look at how we can put into practice two phrases that have become part of our language: 'clearing the air' and 'getting it off our chest'.

Let's look at various people and some situations they found themselves in, often again and again.

The angry employee

Sheila, a graphic designer at a large advertising agency, had no idea what was going on. For no obvious reason, she was constantly annoyed by one of the executives, a quiet, self-contained type. It did not help that she knew this man was well respected in her company. If he just passed her in the corridor and failed to smile warmly, she would tell everyone what a thoroughly unpleasant character he was. From time to time he would drop by her office to congratulate her on doing a good job, but she could never accept the compliment. She either thought that he was being patronising, or that he was being manipulative and wanted something more from her. Her colleagues told her she was being ridiculous, but she 'knew' she could see the real person behind the pleasant mask. She finally had to rethink when her best friend started going out with the man!

The frightened boss

Jack was in his mid-fifties when I first met him, a good-looking, very tall man, who ran his own property development company. As a young man with a large real estate firm, he had climbed very rapidly up the corporate ladder and well before the age of thirty was a senior director. He had a very open and friendly style as a boss, and was liked and trusted. He had one rather large hang-up, though. He was only friendly with men. When faced by a woman, he would become very nervous and start stammering, and, of course, he had many female employees. As for friendships with women, he had never even entertained the possibility. When his company hired a consultant to help their team-building, they began '360s' – an exercise where you receive an assessment from the most senior executive to the most junior assistant. Every man in the company said how fair, personable and warm he was. Every woman, on the other hand, reported how unapproachable he felt and how little respect they had for him. At that point he got a strong wake-up call. Shocked to his core, he came to see me. He knew he could not run his business *and* stay distant from women because of fear.

Lonely Tom

Tom was someone whom very few people could get to know. He worked hard, then drove home to his house in the suburbs and rarely went out. When Ed, an old school friend, got in touch, Tom offered to meet him at a local restaurant. Tom started criticising his old friend immediately for his job, then his car, then his life in general. Ed, remembering a kinder, gentler side, asked him what was going on. Tom sighed deeply and said that no one seemed to like him anymore: 'I don't know what I do, but it seems as if everyone turns against me sooner or later.' Probing, Ed wondered if Tom himself might have something to do with their reaction. Tom denied it at first, but eventually as the evening went on admitted to one thing: 'People take up far too much time. Life's a lot easier without hearing about all their problems.'

Social Sally

Sally was known as the life and soul of the party. In fact, she gave most of the parties in her town and people had come to rely on her to bring them together. After a few years of this, Sally started noticing that she was getting asked out far less than she was playing hostess. 'How come I have to do all the work?' she cried, and started bad-mouthing her former friends for using her. Slowly she dropped most of them and just spent time with her husband and kids.

PATTERN-SPOTTING

You know how we say some people are really good at spotting faults in others, but not so crystal clear when it comes to themselves? Let's do a variation on that. How good are you at spotting patterns now? Try identifying what patterns these people have but are not able to see themselves.

With Sheila, the pattern is not obvious at first. She has gone on the offensive, so what we need to feel is what she might be protecting underneath. Her need is to be seen, recognised and appreciated. It took some humility for her to acknowledge that, but eventually she owned up to it for herself. She called the pattern: 'needing approval'.

What would you say about Jack, the company boss who only felt comfortable with men? Distrust of women? Shyness? Fear of criticism? When I was working with him, we started sifting through his patterns and traced them back to a huge amount of unresolved issues with his mother. She had ruled with terror over his childhood household. He had grown up unable to trust her or even speak to her and had kept those emotional memories buried but still alive all his life. In his work and personal life he kept imposing that image on all other women. The part of his mind that had not grown up was keeping him that small, anxious boy waiting to be criticised or singled out for punishment. The dominant patterns he needed to deal with were just those: Expecting criticism and fearing punishment.

As for Lonely Tom, rather than simply rejecting, perhaps what he is doing is *rejecting before being rejected*. That's the pattern at play. He recreates the loneliness and abandonment he might have felt when much younger. He is not able to adapt to a different environment.

What pattern would you say is going on with Social Sally? Feeling used? Playing victim? Compulsively pleasing being turned into resentment? You play the pattern detective here.

FRIENDSHIP QUESTIONNAIRE

Are you conscious of friendships or work relationships that always end up a certain way? Do you often lose faith in people, or feel distrusting generally? Do you find yourself very critical or – its opposite – always eager to praise? What might there be in your relations with other people that is worth clearing up? Let's have a good look at how you would assess your present life in this area.

Firstly, rate yourself from 1 to 10 on each of these questions.

How easy or difficult is it for you to approach others?
Easy 1 2 3 4 5 6 7 8 9 10 Difficult

How easy or difficult is it for you to trust others?
Easy 1 2 3 4 5 6 7 8 9 10 Difficult

Do you consider yourself more of an open or closed person?
Open 1 2 3 4 5 6 7 8 9 10 Closed

How easy or difficult is it for others to approach you?
Easy 1 2 3 4 5 6 7 8 9 10 Difficult

How easy or difficult is it for others to tell you their problems?
Easy 1 2 3 4 5 6 7 8 9 10 Difficult

How easy or difficult is it for you to let others know how you are feeling?
Easy 1 2 3 4 5 6 7 8 9 10 Difficult

Do you see yourself as having a circle of good friends?
Yes 1 2 3 4 5 6 7 8 9 10 No

How often do you feel lonely?
Never 1 2 3 4 5 6 7 8 9 10 Often

How many times in your life you have 'fallen out' with good friends?
Never 1 2 3 4 5 6 7 8 9 10 Often

How did you score? Add up your totals.

If you scored between:
- 64 and 90, you probably find making relationships very difficult. Be aware of patterns like 'distrust', withdrawal', 'shut down', 'loner' and 'rejecting before being rejected'.
- 40 and 63, you do not find it difficult being around people, but they tend to be more acquaintances than friends. You find it hard to stay in healthy friendships. Be aware of patterns like 'disappointed', 'easily bored', 'high expectations', 'lack of commitment' and the message that 'the grass is always greener on the other side'.
- 8 and 39, you have an easy time making and keeping friends. If your life is dedicated to healthy change, be open to learning even more about responsible communication.

Remember each time you find some patterns, you can work through them with the steps of the process. After becoming aware of them, trace their origin to realise that you learned them, and that they are not inherently yours. Express any old charge you may have around them, and forgive yourself and the person you might have learned the pattern from. Then you can learn and practice new behaviour.

AWARENESS: UNDERSTANDING OUR REACTIONS TO OTHER PEOPLE

Having looked at your current life, what would you like to change in your day-to-day relationships? If you believe that this part of your life could do with some more light thrown on it, begin by doing some sleuth work on your relationships at work and with friends. See if there are patterns that continue to recur. What gets you fired up or makes you lose patience? Who do you tend to brush off quickly? Whose approval do you need?

Do you remember situations when you have had a *strong* reaction to a friend or work colleague? They have been over-bearing or energy-sucking, over-protective or uncaring. It could even go back to the first sight you had of them. Perhaps they looked so in control of things that you 'knew' they wouldn't give you the time of day. You protected yourself by deciding to dislike them before they could make that decision about you! Or they appeared so needy you reckoned it would be best to avoid them.

REACTIONS

Use this list to put down some of your reactions:

Person:
_____

Reactions:
_____

Situation:
_____

My perception of them:
_____

My reaction to them (patterns):
_____

Be brief here. For example: Steve. On the phone this morning. I perceived him to be cold and distant. I reacted by thinking 'Why bother?' Underneath, the pattern was 'feeling excluded'.

You may have even given up trying to change because by

now things seem to be set in stone. 'A leopard doesn't change its spots,' my father would say. Anyway, you tell yourself, even if *I* change, they won't (the pattern here is 'not trusting others'!)

Repairing a friendship

Once, teaching a residential course, I kept thinking that one of the other teachers was interrupting me. I started noticing, I thought, that she was correcting me and clarifying the theory or instructions that I was explaining at the time. A couple of days of this, and I was entertaining some less-than-pleasant thoughts about her. I felt undermined, as if her comments were implying that I was not good enough to hold my own at the front of the room. Strangely, this was not someone I had just met. This was Cynthia, one of my closest friends and colleagues, with whom I had trained, taught my first courses and travelled overseas. She had even been a witness at my wedding. I really liked her, normally. So what was going on?

I asked if she would come and help me clear up the issue, before I looked daggers at her or launched an attack in front of everyone else! I sat down and first acknowledged to myself the feelings I was having and my wish to resolve the situation. My heart was racing and my face felt very warm. Since she trusted that my intention was to clear the air, she gave me her permission to go ahead.

'Cynthia,' I said, 'there have been times these last few days when I have been feeling upset. I perceived you to be interrupting me or trying to make clearer what I had been saying; for example in the instructions for writing. I thought that you wanted to take over and sound better than me. I reacted with the patterns of feeling angry and shutting down to you.'

I fell silent for a couple of moments. Then I said to her, 'You know what, Cynthia. I really value our friendship and I appreciate what a very kind and generous friend you are.'

She looked back at me, smiled, and said, 'Thanks for letting me know that. I thought there was something coming between us recently, but I couldn't put my finger on it.'

With that, the charge was gone and the rest of the time we were back to our normal state of friendship.

Recognising that part of our minds, the aspect of our inner childlike Emotional self, is caught up in the past, helps us build a healthy bridge to the present. That's the first part.

EXPRESSION:
COMMUNICATING AND LETTING GO

Having detected the patterns affecting your relationships, the next step is to do something about them. Imagine what a gift it might be to offer yourself the opportunity not only to own a charge from the past but then also to communicate it directly in a safe and non-judgmental atmosphere.

For this to work, choose someone whom you feel will understand why you are doing this, and what type of language will be used. Remind your friend or colleague that their role as listener is merely to receive without responding. You are the one taking responsibility for any leftovers from the past.

If it feels right, having gentle eye contact often dispels the old reaction, as you see the other person for who they really are, not as how you perceived them to be. Eyes, those 'windows of the soul', reveal the heart beneath the screen on to which we've projected our old movies.

Standing as an equal, you are able to feel stronger. Then when you speak, the internal emotions are brought to the surface, and those old feelings become less and less powerful until they are gone.

When you feel ready, prepare the same exercise I went through with my colleague and friend Cynthia (see page 165).

Refer to the steps on page 152 then look at these:

RESPONSIBLE COMMUNICATION

1. Make sure your intention is to resolve a friendship.
2. Use 'I' statements. Make clear it's you who's talking.
3. Name the situation – be specific, not 'you always' or 'you never'.
4. Name the feeling – anger, sadness, concern, upset, etc.
5. Call your own pattern – for example, 'abandoned', 'ignored', 'victim'.
6. Appreciate the qualities of the other person.

There are of course many situations where it would simply not be appropriate to speak directly to the person. If you live with someone or are a very close friend, you have the time and the space to work things through. But at work this honesty might rather slow down your career path; with a casual acquaintance you might be very misunderstood. However, even in those cases you can take responsibility for what you have felt and be able to move beyond it. You break the energy in the pattern by becoming conscious of exactly what is going on for you.

So, instead of risking it directly with another person, you can *imagine* them opposite you, as in the case study below. Doing this still has a very powerful effect on the way we think and react. You will be able to claim your own power back by understanding that change can happen once your perception of reality changes.

A sense of rejection

Rafaella, a normally vibrant Italian, had been having a lot of problems with her supervisor in a photography shop. She had admired her supervisor greatly, but always at a distance, thinking that she would never have the patience to explain to Rafaella how things worked in the office.

Sitting in a chair with another chair representing her colleague opposite, Rafaella was very hesitant at first. It was hard for her to get the words out: '. . . I felt rejected by you because I thought you looked down on me.' During the whole time she was trying to say this, she was hardly breathing. I noticed her begin to actually shake with fear. When I asked her about it, she said that it was the fear she always felt inside when she felt a deep rejection. It was the fear that she kept down which made her physically ill – a deep self-sabotage.

Afterwards she expressed her anger and frustration at the pattern she named: 'feeling rejected'. She had not worked on it before and it took her days to face it. She did not notice an immediate effect but something deep must have shifted. She called a few weeks later and told me, 'There have been several occasions recently where normally I would have definitely experienced that feeling of rejection, but each time I still felt OK. I don't experience the old tightness in my chest anymore.'

Forgiveness for old friends

You can also use the methods of this process of change to heal an old friendship that has turned bitter. Sometimes our best friends become our worst enemies, especially if there is fear and greed around money involved. However much you feel the other person has hurt you, check out any patterns in you that might have prevented you from remaining their friend. You could look for pride, or insensitivity and stubbornness, for example. Then make a list of the patterns with which you feel they acted. They might have been 'cold', 'manipulative' or 'having to be right'. Now – here's the twist – which of their patterns could you acknowledge as ones that you have ever had? This takes some humility. In particular, the pattern of 'having to be right' is a difficult one to admit. But if you manage to make that connection, you are halfway down the road to rescuing the relationship. You have seen that as human beings you are more similar to than different from this former friend.

Remember how we worked with *Forgiveness* in Part One of this book? First look for some understanding as to how they developed their patterns in the first place. Remind yourself that they are their learned patterns. Again, you do not have to condone their behaviour as adults, but you can learn to forgive the person underneath. Forgiveness, whether in your imagination or in person, will let you step out of the rut you have been caught in.

If you feel that you are able to forgive this former friend, then go to them bearing a gift as a symbol of peace. It could be some flowers, a book or a simple piece of art. Whether or not you express words of forgiveness to them, do not ask or even expect them to take responsibility for their part, though hearing your changed attitude, they may well do just that. You cannot expect to change anyone but yourself. A healing can occur simply because you have laid down your arms and softened your heart.

NEW BEHAVIOUR: GIVING AND RECEIVING FEEDBACK

Think of the following as a very valuable 'New Behaviour'. Imagine that you and the people you associated with had the courage to speak the truth about your reactions. The first time would be very scary. You have to remember the intention, which is to clear the air and repair the relationship. Keep in mind the fact that you care enough about this relationship to take it to another level. Until now, the hurdle, or barrier, has been the old rule, learned when we were children: 'Don't say what you really feel'. What's more, the only 'feedback' we ever got might have been in the form of criticism from a parent: 'You're too untidy'; 'Could you take more effort in your appearance'; 'You look like a slut'; 'No one's interested. Now be quiet'. But that was then, and this is now. The past is over.

Our society does not put a high value on honest disclosure. It's as if we all are walking around holding a banner that says: 'Don't tell me anything too revealing about myself, and I won't say anything "bad" about you.' So, not daring to let our friends know that we are bothered by an aspect of their behaviour, or that we have a hard time with our own reactions, we keep our relationships on a safe but superficial level.

What might you learn if ever you found yourself in the position of listening to someone taking responsibility for their reaction to *you*? You may of course find yourself not reacting. You do not identify with their reaction because you know it's not *you* this person is talking about.

On the other hand, if it does push a button with you, or if

you receive the same kind of reaction again and again, you need to consider how your behaviour might lead to these reactions. If the mud sticks, examine it.

Staying in control

Björn, who worked in an engineering company, was aware that he was not well accepted by his colleagues, but did not know why. When we did a clearing exercise at his firm, one or two of them said they found him cold and off-putting. Björn was at first able to disassociate from their reactions on an intellectual level, telling himself that it was all their stuff. But after a few more said the same thing, he really started listening. No longer defensive, he commented, 'It was shocking to realise how I presented myself at the company, if so many people had the same reaction. They were actually frightened of me and tried to keep out of my way.'

Björn realised that this played itself out in all areas of his life, and he had escaped behind it to avoid becoming emotionally close to people. It was safer to stay in control and was exactly how his father had gone through life. It seemed to 'function' in his workplace, but it was taking a real toll on his family. His teenaged kids were growing up not knowing who he was, and his wife had pretty much given up trying to break through his defences. Hearing that other people had the same reactions helped melt this armour plating at a time when he was feeling very alone inside that armour. He began to let people in, though he needed a few coaching sessions to make his initial appearance seem less severe and more inviting to people.

RESPONSIBLE LISTENING

If you find yourself in a situation of receiving feedback, and are interested in learning and changing, then follow these steps.

1. Before you begin, make sure your intention is to take responsibility for your part in the situation, not to defend yourself.
2. Do not interrupt. You are just listening.
3. Show that you are listening – keep your body language open, and maintain eye contact.
4. When you believe the other person has finished, make sure by asking them if there is anything else they want to add.
5. Let them know you have heard what they said by briefly paraphrasing their words.
6. Ask them if they are willing to hear from you.
7. Acknowledge your part in the situation. Talk about your feelings. Watch the temptation to be right at this stage!
8. Finally, thank the other person for caring about your friendship enough to want to clear this up with you.

It's better to be seen

Macey felt very ignored in her company. When no one came up to clear any incidents with her during a team-training day, the penny dropped. She felt invisible. She realised, of course, that this was exactly the role she had been playing all her life. It hurt her to be ignored by people who she was working alongside every day. The pressure to say something built up so much that she felt pulled to her feet by some outside force and found herself saying, to all there, 'Hey, what about me? I exist, too.' She let them know exactly what was going on with her, standing on her own in the middle of the room. She remembers that moment, coming out of her own shell, as simply terrifying: 'But to be able to state my claim for my own life was a huge personal breakthrough. No one ignored me after that!'

As human beings, we all want to be seen and listened to. We want to be acknowledged. The truth is that most of us *want* to be told about what might be getting in the way of a friendship. That way we figure as important in someone's life.

We're noticed. If we're never told anything, it's possibly because we are seen as protecting ourselves with an image of being good or perfect. It could also be that we're seen as so fragile, that no one would want to hurt us. Ultimately we lose out: no one can get too close.

One of life's occupational hazards is that patterns keep emerging. It's all too easy to colour other people with our image of them. Themes that recur again and again might be to see older people as figures of authority, shaven-headed teenagers as figures of fear, men as protectors and women as nurturers, attractive people as unobtainable, and foreigners as 'people we don't trust'. Once you realise that these are knee-jerk reactions to a conditioned belief from the past, you can own them for yourself and use them as a self-learning process. It could even help you break a life-long pattern. We *all* want to be liked, respected and loved for who we are. Yes, even your boss has those normal human feelings! We just have to remember that and keep our hearts open so that others can touch it and be touched by it.

THE GIFT OF APPRECIATION

We might find hearing other people's reactions difficult. We may be hopeless, though, at going beyond that to actually appreciating each other – or ourselves. You can also change this pattern, but you need to practise something different!

Firstly, what do you value in yourself? What are you most proud of? What do you imagine your friends would say about you to others? Only their positive comments are allowed here! It may be that you're loyal, or generous, or funny, or playful, or have a mischievous spirit. Take some time to reflect on those qualities. Let them in and hold them in your heart. Only when you've filled up your own cup are you ready to pour some love and appreciation into someone else's.

Next, go and find someone who you value and would like to appreciate. Make this a time when you can be fully *present* to the other person. It may be hard if it's the office, so choose a time of day when things have usually quietened down. (If there are various reasons why it would be hard to do in person, then *imagine* appreciating this person. The power of thought is strong enough to change a relationship. They will still sense that your attitude has changed somehow, even if they cannot put their finger on what is different).

Look at the other person and start with 'I appreciate you for . . .' It does not have to be too long, or too 'sacred', especially if the other person looks uncomfortable. Remember how it was for you to find qualities in yourself.

Afterwards, meditate for a moment on how it was to

give an appreciation. I bet it made you feel better, as it must have done the person receiving. It's as if part of our brain believes we're hearing it for ourselves when we utter those words. If you are clearing up any issues with a friend, do end with the gift of appreciation.

CHALLENGING YOUR FRIENDS TO CHANGE

Being told something about ourselves can be hard to take because we fear criticism or judgement. Because most of us were brought up with this, it makes receiving not only compliments but also suggestions very daunting. So how do you imagine it is for other people? Exactly. It's not easy. They, just like us, would far prefer to play safe, and keep everything nice and polite. But that way we keep the same old status quo. Nothing changes and no one grows.

Until now we have been working on our own patterns and have learned about receiving feedback by listening without judgement. Here's a chance to be the agent of change for someone else. It may break a pattern of theirs, and it will certainly break one of yours about confidence and speaking your mind. First, follow this exercise to get in touch with what you might like to say to someone whose friendship you enjoy.

THE CHALLENGE TO CHANGE

- *First Impression*: Do you remember the first time that you met this person? What did you think at the time? Did you find them approachable or rather off-putting, energetic or depressed, lonely or sociable?
- *Present Impression*: What do you think of them now? Do you feel they have changed, or has your impression of them changed?
- *Challenge*: Do you ever wonder what would be an interesting challenge for them? Do you see them reading less and dancing more, staying in less and going out more? Or being quieter and less sociable? Is there anything concrete you can think of that could challenge them, like a mountain to climb or a salsa class to join?
- *Expression*: If you want to take this next step, to 'Expression', tell this good friend that you would like to try something out with them. Say it will only take five minutes and it will be fun. Let them know first that this is going to be about how you used to see them and how you see them at the present time. They may be amused to hear your first impressions now that you are good friends. Next, tell them what you think of them today. It could be a wonderful appreciation. Finally, if it feels right – they may still be absorbing what you have just said – ask if you might make a couple of suggestions.

Inspired to change

Alison, an executive search consultant, told me about being on the receiving end of this once. She was really scared. She suddenly felt in the hot seat, imagining that her friend Katherine was going to say something awful about her. To her great surprise, what Katherine said was wholly positive.

Alison felt really acknowledged. She heard how warm, courageous and humorous she was. Her friend even said that Alison had inspired her to be courageous herself. 'I realised that in the past I was so afraid of receiving any feedback because of the constant criticism I got as a child. I have *never* been able to take compliments. As soon as someone said anything remotely nice I would undermine it, or brush it off. So listening to this really liberated something in me. I began to realise that feedback is not about criticism, but about positive observation that can help me develop.'

When you make a suggestion about how a friend can change, you are widening the parameters of your relationship. You have also given permission for them to suggest challenges for you, too. So beware – don't use this unless you're also prepared to be challenged!

If you can become aware of and then drop old conditioned reactions you will find your whole world changing. Instead of a place in which you imagine criticism and distrust, it becomes one of learning and acceptance. Like a knight who takes off his chain mail, you can then walk around freely, enjoying your environment and the people who share it with you. You have realised the truth that you no longer need the chain mail of old patterns to protect you.

Knowing yourself much better, being able to keep your personal and professional relationships clear and open to feedback, appreciation and suggestions, you will be in a great position to follow your own path of change. With more open and trusting friends and work colleagues, you will be around people who value your honesty. They will support you growing and developing. You will find that it is no accident those people are in your current life.

11

Choose Your Work. Don't Let it Choose You

We work to become, not to acquire.

ESTHER HUBBARD

Carl, a retail shop manager, shoved the pile of bills out of his way as he made for the front door in the early morning. 'Another day at the salt mines,' he muttered to himself on his way out. When I bumped into him later that day at a café, and we started talking about our lives, I asked him what he thought of the phrase, 'Work like you don't need the money.'

'Ha, Ha, very funny,' was his immediate reply. 'I can count on the fingers of one hand the number people who are working for love rather than money. We've all got serious bills to pay now.'

Is that true for you? Are you happy with your work or does it just pay the bills? Are you content with how you are spending your forty or more hours a week? Would you say that you are driven by passion rather than duty? Do you feel challenged and well rewarded? Do you feel that you are creating something useful? On a scale of one to ten, how satisfied are you with your occupation?

If you feel less than totally satisfied by your work, perhaps you did not choose what you do, but rather fell into it by accident. Do you now try to gloss over your compromised dreams, telling yourself, 'This is the best I'll get. It may not be great, but at least I'm working'?

Most people have some things about their working life that they would like to change. In this chapter we'll be looking at patterns around work and money and how to make the most out of our innate talents.

PATTERN DETECTIVE

It's time to play pattern detective again. Look at the patterns and messages you might have stored up inside.
Tick any boxes that apply to you

- [ ] workaholic/obsessed by work
- [ ] work just pays the bills
- [ ] feel unimportant/unappreciated
- [ ] feel trapped in a job
- [ ] stressed out/burned out
- [ ] take on too many commitments
- [ ] work is most important thing in life
- [ ] work is more important than family and friends
- [ ] devalue success/achievement
- [ ] lack initiative
- [ ] overly ambitious
- [ ] abuse power of position
- [ ] never accept responsibility
- [ ] play power games
- [ ] perfectionist/never satisfied
- [ ] frequently lose jobs/get fired
- [ ] fear of failure
- [ ] fear of success

What have you found out about yourself and your attitudes to work? If you can acknowledge your own patterns with honesty, then you can start taking down the bricks that make up your own walls. If they are patterns that particularly frustrate you, you might need to do some expressive work around them. At the very least, write them down with some notes on how fed up you are.

Obsessed by work

Steve, a director of a large insurance company, realised that he had become obsessed by work when, on a beach holiday with his family, his young kids asked him why he had brought down so much paperwork with him. As he looked at the piles of financial reports in their rented villa, he wondered how work had managed to take over his family life and even his ability to take a break. What's more, it seemed as if the next thirty or more years were mapped out. He had his mortgage to pay, his pension to plan, and his kids to educate. But even though he was well paid, there never seemed to be enough money. He sank into a depression because he no longer felt any control, or any joy in his life. He felt trapped.

Steve was eventually able to change his obsession with work and his depression about feeling trapped. His colleagues saw that change as so remarkable that they now refer to 'old Steve' and 'new Steve'. He had been sitting on so much stress that when he began consciously to let it go in a safe setting, he exploded in tears and rage. With that tension out of his mind and body, he became much more open to new ideas and far more relaxed about how things were done. He trusted that the managers under him would do things capably and efficiently, rather than expecting them to mess up. As a result, of course, the *whole* atmosphere in the office around him became more relaxed and open to new ways.

Our attitudes to work are rapidly changing. Ironically, while the developed world has never been wealthier, we are spending more and more time at work rather than using this wealth to enjoy our leisure. It is through work that people are now defining their social roles. Asking someone on first meeting 'What work do you do?' used to be considered in bad taste. Now it would be strange not to. It's 'who we are' that seems to matter. We use a phrase like, 'I'm so busy now, I'm rushed off my feet,' when in fact we are in control, to suggest that we're successful. We're saying that we're successful. We're wanted. To admit that we're taking it easy or have time on our hands means that we've somehow failed our responsibilities. We have this implicit agreement that none of us will step off the great treadmill of life.

Because of the speed and the many interactions and demands at work, more and more people are stating that home life feels dull in comparison. On top of that, they complain that they don't feel important back at home. Their self-worth depends on their work and the money they earn. How did it come to be this way?

Society creates norms and we all try to fit in. The norm in our developed world is to work hard and make good money. It may not be the same in the South Pacific, and so we cannot say it's innate in us humans. If our lives feel empty and meaningless we have to stop and take a good look around at what we have created.

WORK HEALTH CHECK

To examine our working lives in finer detail, let's check in with the four aspects of our being, the Quadrinity.

- Emotionally, how do you feel about your work life? Happy and contented, or sad, depressed and easily irritated? Perhaps even burned-out? Think of the part of you that likes to be childlike, fun and spontaneous. How fulfilled does this part feel?

- Intellectually, how do you feel about work? Are you challenged, learning new things, around stimulating people and ideas? Or are you doing the same thing over and over again? You've learned it well and could go through your working week on auto-pilot. Perhaps your mind is over-active and starting to be over-stressed.

- Is there a balance between what you want your mind to be stimulated by and what your childlike, emotional nature finds interesting? Children get so occupied with their games that they are said to be completely 'in flow'. Time and distractions do not exist. Are there times at work when you are completely 'in flow'? If not, what is it that still gets you excited? Could you bring some of that to your working life?

- Spiritually, do you feel in harmony with your higher vision and purpose? Do you ask God or a Higher Power for guidance in working matters? Do you feel in this respect that you'll be leaving the world a richer place?

- Physically, what is your body telling you about your work? Do you go off with a bounce in your step and feel uplifted throughout the day? Work can have a dramatic effect on health. Most heart attacks occur between eight and nine on a Monday morning. It's called 'parking lot syndrome'. Have you noticed any physical symptoms that might be due to work – recurring headaches or indigestion or a bad back? Do you often feel tired, or find it difficult to sleep?

With all that information available to you, are you ready to start getting at the roots of what you need to change?

CHANGING YOUR WORK LIFE

Do you feel that you *can* make a change in your work life? For instance, you may have long harboured a dream to set up your own business but not got up the courage. What's stopping you? It's natural to have some trepidation before a challenge like this, but it probably goes deeper than just the fear of taking that step. We need to get at the roots, which lie in our family background. By digging them out, we can be free to move off in our own direction.

If it's difficult to imagine making a change, first think back to what messages and beliefs you picked up about work while you were growing up. Did you notice that your father spent more time at work than with the family? That may have set you up to believe that work is more important than you, the family, or indeed anything. Did he stay in the same job or area of work, even though he complained about it? As a result, you may never have questioned your ability to change work, learning that you simply put up with a situation. In fact you may not have challenged the 'rule book' on work as it all seemed so indelibly written into your family's belief system.

If you are finding patterns already amid the set of messages and beliefs, make a note to yourself to work them through in the following way. Once you have connected with an emotional charge around a pattern of, say, frustration or anger or resentment, choose a method of Expression to release it. By now you may have discovered that, as a method of expression, pillow bashing works for you, or running, or dancing, or simply writing it down in a journal.

Focus on one pattern at a time and bring all your attention to building a healthy boundary between it and you: 'Enough,' you might shout, 'I don't want this in my life anymore.' With the charge released, you will find the pattern's grip on you weakened, or indeed completely broken. A change of belief is needed to start making actual changes in your work life.

To plant the seed for further changes, think back to what type of outfit your father and mother (if she worked) were part of. Was it a small or large business, a family concern or a huge multinational? Did they work in the private or public sector? Were they employed in industry, services, finances or academia? Now, what about you . . . ? Do you see similarities in your work situation? Perhaps their work place might even have predetermined yours. If you're dissatisfied in your present situation, here's what you can do to shake things up. Get in touch with the emotional charge you have around it. Then express it. Get it out of you. Not only are you healing the conflict inside about how or where you work, but you are also 'giving back' the message that says you have to lead life this way. You might have observed certain attitudes about work when you were growing up, but there's no need for them to be carried forward into your adult life.

There may well be advantages to a certain type of upbringing when it comes to finding a job that you might never have considered an asset. Janine, who works in an employment agency, told me how she interviews people for jobs in sales. 'I ask them what their standard of living was like when they were growing up. If they say they were pretty hard up, I know that they'll be "hungrier" and will work harder to get a sale. If they never knew any hardship, they're likely to be too relaxed!' In the same way, the sons and daughters of risk-taking entrepreneurs are often ones to start up their own business. If you have healthy roots, nourish them. They will grow and bear fruit for you.

If you are feeling stuck and discontented in your working life, and have absolutely no idea why, let's take a trip down on the elevator to find out what's keeping you there and what you can do about it.

THE ELEVATOR

The question to ask yourself is: *What are the patterns preventing me from feeling fulfilled at work?* Then just hold this question in your mind for now. You can choose your own words for a question if you wish to make it more personal.

Imagine an elevator in front of you. Step into it, and see on the control panel a button marked with your question. Push that button and feel the elevator start to go down. Feel yourself going down seven levels, down through the years and various levels of your consciousness, until the elevator stops, the doors open, and you walk out. It's a scene or a picture or some kind of insight into the past. Look around you. What's happening? Who's there? What are you doing? What might you be learning?

Look at Sylvia's case history, below. When you do this exercise in this way, you are changing the internal script by which your life is run. You can then take that further and change your actual environment. It may be that you will see the need to simplify your life. I have personally never met anyone who wanted to work in a larger office or spend more time at a desk! If that is the case with you, what small step could you take today to make that dream closer to a reality?

What work really means

Sylvia imagined herself travelling down into the past. When the doors of the elevator opened, she found herself visiting her father's office as a small girl of around seven. Her father's desk was much smaller than she had imagined and was surrounded by more than twenty others in a room full of computer screens and telephones. Her father looked rather embarrassed. Sylvia felt awkward seeing her father that way.

Diagnosing what she might have got from that learning window, Sylvia said that she picked up two things. One was a sense that work was not to be enjoyed. The other was that at work you would just be one cog in a machine along with many others.

I asked her if she wanted to go down again and get a different script by which to live life. She said she certainly did. This time, she imagined walking up to her father and saying, 'Why don't we go to the boss's office?' They both went into the plush room in the corner of the building. It had great views. They sat down with the boss for a chat. In this scene, Sylvia asked the boss if her father could do something different. The boss said that in truth her father was not best used there. He should go off and become a consultant to another organisation. They would pay better and he would rise up the organisation quicker.

'How do you know that?' asked Sylvia.

'Because I'm going over there myself', said the boss.

Still in her imagination, Sylvia turned to her Dad and said, 'Hand in your notice.'

Seeing it like this showed Sylvia that she didn't need to stay forever in a job herself. Afterwards, she needed help not just in finding the courage but also in 'selling herself' into a new job. We worked together on her vision at the same time as her self-confidence, until the day when she landed a dream job combining a love of art with her business expertise as manager of an animation studio.

CHANGING OUR ATTITUDES TO LEADERSHIP

Leaders don't force people to follow – they invite them on a journey.
CHARLES LAUER

If you are comfortable communicating your needs with your boss you are probably able to make effective changes in your life. You do not wait for things just to happen to you. But take that a step further and consider *being* a boss. How would that feel? Of course, you will be well rewarded. Being at ease with your own power of authority means that society – and especially the business world – will shower you with money and prestige. Those who rise to this challenge are few, perhaps because we associate it with 'sticking our heads above the parapet' and so being a target. In Australia they call it the 'tall poppy syndrome'. If you stand above the other poppies, you will get cut down to the level of the crowd. The moral is: stay mediocre and you will fit in. So are *you* prepared to stand out?

Of course, there are other issues that come in to play around being a leader. The ability to give clear instructions, to motivate people, to define clear targets and to see opportunities are among some of the positive attributes required. But remember some underlying factors: those who make good leaders are not troubled by authority issues. Those who always question and distrust authority may never make good leaders.

WHAT'S HOLDING YOU BACK?

Let's have a look and see if there are any patterns that might be preventing you from taking more of a leadership role. If you would like to have more authority at work, you cannot be in denial about what you feel and believe beneath the surface. Tick or mentally note which of these boxes might apply to you. Then later we can set about changing them.
Patterns around Authority:

- fear of authority
- hate authority
- submissive/compliant/easily give in
- have to have authority/'I'm the boss here'
- undermine authority
- divisive – 'us against them'

Left over from our family background and reinforced by school, many of us have deeply held negative attitudes to authority. They're the bad guys. By keeping ourselves as underdogs, we can at least retain a sense of pride. We *need* them to stand against.

To many, authority is to be feared and obeyed. Through this

fear, we lose our own sense of authority and the ability to 'author' our own lives. We submit to someone who has more power, money or status and forget we have a right of reply. Due to our own lack of self-esteem, coupled with probably strong family patterns about giving in to our parents, we become followers.

The other side of being fearful or distrustful of leaders, however, is the pattern of 'overwielding authority'. Good leaders are like good parents. They believe in and trust those they have around them. They empower their followers to learn and develop their own way of doing things. They *serve* rather than using their position to feel that they are better and more powerful than others.

Bad leaders, just like parents, can abuse their position and become bullies. Never sure that they are themselves liked and trusted, they use tactics of intimidation to get their objectives met. They lecture rather than explain and threaten rather than persuade.

Did your parents model good leadership when you were growing up? Claire, a local councillor, said that her father, a well-known national politician, was so tired when he came home that he just shouted at people. He took his frustrations out on his family. What made her so upset was seeing how admired he was when out meeting his constituents. 'If only you knew,' she thought to herself. Of course, following the path of least resistance, she copied his tyrannical ways until a deep self-loathing told her it was time to do something about it.

What we lose out on is becoming a good leader at some point ourselves. If we keep submitting to, or fighting our conditioned beliefs, then we are not truly independent to lead our lives for ourselves. Just as if we were children all over again. By resolving these issues, we can transcend them. Hopefully we can do this before we have leadership thrust upon us simply by growing older and more experienced. To clear them out, follow the steps of the process of change. Once you are aware of the roots of your behaviour, express the charge around it in some way. Let out the internalised emotion that binds the pattern. The emotion holding the pattern could just as easily be shame, fear or frustration. If you feel a very strong influence of one parent or another on you, in your mind let them know that it's *their* pattern or belief, not yours. Build a boundary between them and you. Once you have discharged the energy around the pattern, forgive yourself, and this parent or carer, whatever may have been the mistakes of the past. If you need more help with this stage, look back at Chapter Six. With that completed, you can start building New Behaviour.

In two minds about leadership

If you have conflicting views about leadership and authority, have a dialogue between your Emotional self and your Intellect to see what is going on inside. At the same time you could enquire what would be satisfying and interesting to both. I tried this with Lauren, a researcher in a pharmaceutical company. This is what her two parts said:

Emotional self: I hate being told what to do!

Intellect: We need to accept orders from senior management. How else are we going to keep a job?

Emotional self: Oh, come on, this is no way to live. We never get to choose what to do.

Intellect: That may be so, but we make a lot of money.

Emotional self: So what? I can't feel it. It doesn't make me feel any better.

Intellect: Have you got any suggestions about what we might do differently?

> *Emotional self*: Well, firstly, I wonder if you might ask to take on more responsibility. I have a really creative side, and I know I could contribute that to others, if we were in a position where people would listen.
>
> *Intellect*: Hmmm. Well, if you agreed to really be on my side, and give up that underdog role of yours, I'd be very happy to do that. It just could work.
>
> *Emotional self*: Great. Let's go and talk to someone about it!
>
> Lauren applied for a more senior role and was offered not one, but three different positions. She was able to move out over the walls she had built around herself.

You too can change your situation when you have expressed self-defeating patterns or when you have resolved a conflict between your emotional and intellectual sides. By reworking the script that determines your old reaction, you will find yourself responding in different ways altogether. As a result, you may be prompted to leave a work situation once you have seen how unsuitable it is for you. You may start changing your job description by communicating your needs. You will not just have seen but also felt that you do not need to put up with the way things have been. You can be the foremost author of change in your own life.

CHANGING OUR ATTITUDES TO MONEY

It's not just a fear of authority that makes us stay in jobs to which we are not suited. In most cases it stems from a fear that we won't survive if we leave our safe and secure position – the pattern of 'fear of poverty'. 'How will we ever make a living?'

we ask ourselves. The fear of not having any money then gets rationalised by our Intellect – 'It's not so easy getting a job these days' – and we stay where we are, comfortably miserable.

The funny thing is that the other side of the coin may also be a pattern we need to look at – a 'fear of abundance'. We are so used to living life in a limited way that we may very well have a belief that we do not deserve to have a plentiful supply of money. Money provides many more choices about how to live. What if we just do not want to deal with all the choices that come with that money?

It's the same principle that makes us put up with dead-end relationships. *The fear of change is greater than the change itself.*

WHAT DOES MONEY MEAN TO YOU?

Would you like to find out more about how money works in your life? First, look at this list of patterns and messages and tick or make a mental note of which ones apply to you.

- [ ] 'Money will take care of everything'
- [ ] Always spending
- [ ] Always in debt
- [ ] Save money compulsively
- [ ] Fear of poverty
- [ ] Fear of abundance
- [ ] Materialistic
- [ ] Need expensive things to feel OK
- [ ] Compulsively buy presents
- [ ] Devalue importance of money
- [ ] Manipulate through money
- [ ] Dominate through money
- [ ] Worried about the money I have now
- [ ] 'Make a lot of money'

If love of money is the root of all evil, there are a lot of deep roots around now. We worship money. The phrase, 'They've got loads of money' has an almost magical power to it these days. It is given so much importance because we are out of touch with our deeper, inner values.

Many people value their financial worth higher than their self-worth.

Quadrinity check

Let's do a Quadrinity check around money to see how it can affect all parts of our being and what we might first need to change.

Emotionally: Do you get to enjoy it? Does your childlike nature get to play with it – to go out and celebrate, or to reward yourself with what you (not the fashion and lifestyle magazines) decide are quality items? Or do you hoard it? Perhaps it's hard for you ever to treat yourself, and you live by phrases such as 'Put it away for a rainy day' and postpone buying something you want until it gets discounted.

Up until recently the title for stingiest man in the world, according to the *Guinness Book of World Records*, went to a man who invited himself to the funerals of people he had never met so that he could get a free meal. The current holder washes his dental floss after use, dries it, and saves himself up to US$3.50 each year.

Hopefully you'll never go that far but do you compulsively save, out of fear that there will never be enough?

The other extreme is to believe money will buy friends, happiness, power and success. It may look like you're successful if you splash out on a smart new car and move to a 'better' neighbourhood, but what does it feel like inside? What pleasure is it giving your emotional self? Therapist rooms all over the world are filled with 'successful' people feeling completely empty.

A friend of mine used to work as a butler to one of the world's wealthiest men. This was a man who travelled with a large entourage and had palatial homes all over the world. His enormous private yacht had its own support ship and his jet was always standing by with crew at the nearest airport. 'So how was he with all of that?' I asked. 'Bored' was my friend's one-word reply. If you look at the stories of people who have won the lottery, time after time the huge payouts have only brought them greater loneliness and sorrow as they lose their old friends and values.

How can you use money to satisfy yourself emotionally? Think of ways to have fun and enjoy life more. You may need to start investigating ways to play again! Neil gave up his big Mercedes and his highly stressful public relations career when he realised how unsatisfied he was. Life had seemed like an endless series of 'big meetings' with 'major deadlines'. He had become more and more impatient and cynical. He finally quit when his wife, who he had known since he was fifteen, asked him when he had lost his sense of humour. He took out his savings to start a hot-air ballooning company and, though he works long hours, he loves what he does. For him the hours don't matter as it's no longer 'work'.

Intellectually: What do you use money for? Do you enrol on courses to learn more? Do you buy books about subjects that interest you? Do you go travelling to find out more about the many different cultures in the world? Have you joined clubs or societies that cater for your common interests? Does money help stimulate your interest in life-long learning? Think what you might do to use money more, well, intelligently.

Physically: Does your money get used on your body? A massage, a trip to a warm ocean, a set of relaxing bath oils?

Does your body get recognised in the money stakes? You pay for car insurance – do you pay anything to 'insure' your body against disease? Awareness is good, but action is better. Book yourself in for a massage or call that travel agent right now!

Spiritually: There are also spiritual laws around money. Are you recycling the energy that comes your way? If you have been blessed by money, are you helping others who are less fortunate? Our money can make a large difference. You may not feel well off, but put it in perspective. According to the United Nations, 830 million people in the world do not even have enough to eat – many more people than are in the whole of the EU and USA combined. What use are you putting your money to? If you have money in the stock market, do you know how the companies you are investing in make their money? If you're always short, maybe you're being tight with yourself.

Look at the attitudes you have to letting money flow through you and back to the Universe. Money is like love, like the air we breathe, like the energy around us. We think it's 'ours' and that it's limited, so we deny ourselves a true feeling of abundance. Instead of being ruled by an old voice inside that limits you, tune in to the voice of your Spiritual self.

Look to balance all aspects of your Quadrinity when it comes to the use of money. Overall, bear in mind how you value your worth. Is it from the inside or the outside? Are you ready to replace 'net worth' with 'self worth'?

YOU CAN'T TAKE IT WITH YOU WHEN YOU DIE

This exercise could really get you motivated to change your working habits. It will put your attitudes to money as well as to work in proper perspective. Imagine a special event. You have jumped forward some years into the future. A group of your family and friends have gathered for a certain occasion. It's the day of your funeral. You may find this macabre, but firstly remember it's just an exercise and, secondly, it's not a complete work of fiction. None of us is going to live forever.

What would you like them to say at the end of your life? What would you like to be remembered for? Would it be what work you did, and what your money was used for? It would probably be sweet memories, those acts of kindness, your warmth and humour, your human being-ness. You would not be remembered so much for whether you had a big house and robust investment portfolio. When you have the scene very clear in your mind, then come out of this imaginary funeral and take a pen and write, or answer these questions in your mind.

- What would I like to be remembered for after I die?
- What will have been my unique contribution at the end of my life?

John, who worked in an insurance company, wanted to be remembered for his sense of humour and his contribution to his local wildlife organisation. Mervyn said he was proudest of his children and the relationship he had with them. Catherine claimed that her contribution would be her book on cookery that had given so many people pleasure. What will *you* leave behind?

VISION OF A NEW WORKING WORLD

It's time to look at what is it that your heart desires. Do this exercise when you have some moments to yourself. Relax by taking a few deep breaths, preferably with your eyes closed so that you shut out other distractions.

Imagine that you're back in your sanctuary, the garden of your soul, a place of great natural beauty. See yourself there, with the sun shining down. It's as if you can even feel yourself being warmed by that sunshine. There may be a slight breeze around you. You smell how wonderfully fresh the air is with its scent of flowers. You feel completely relaxed.

You are feeling very safe and at peace with yourself. You walk around and find a tree to sit by. The grass around it is wonderfully soft. Take a few deeper breaths, letting yourself relax even more.

In this sanctuary, imagine there's someone coming up towards you. Looking closely at the person, you see that it's *you*. It's your Spiritual self, with all your attributes of peace and wisdom. You sense that there is a quiet power inside of you born of thousands of years of experience. There's also an infinite well of love deep within this soul. If you close your eyes now, you can go deeper into this image of yourself. Breathe it in.

Firstly, ask your Spiritual self for a vision of some meaningful work: something that gets you excited when you wake up and leaves you energised at the end of the day. Then, getting more specific, ask what project you could be involved in. Envision it as if it is happening at this very moment in as much detail as possible.

When you clearly see what work you are doing, ask for

a vision of your physical working environment. Where is it that you see yourself working? Is it at home, in an office, in the theatre? Is it in a town or in the country? Give it a physical setting.

Next, ask for a vision of your human work environment. Do you see yourself working alone or as part of a team? Which would you more enjoy? Which would leave you more fulfilled? How do you get your fun at work?

Unless you are following the desires of your heart, you will not be bringing your energies fully to living your life.

What small step can you take towards that vision today, this week? Even one phone call can get things moving. Craig, a journalist, decided he wanted to teach. All he first needed to do was call a friend who was delighted to have Craig stand in for him at his local adult education college. Just being there at the front of the room allowed Craig to pull an old dream out, rather than keeping it buried under a pile of broken promises. From there he picked up more classes until he got a regular slot.

Remember, if you keep going in the same direction, you'll end up the way you're headed. So choose your direction now if you're not using your full potential. Visioning that direction is wonderful, but walking down it is even more rewarding!

ACTION PLAN FOR CHANGE

The way to change your working life involves these four steps.

Firstly, be *aware* of any patterns you have around work.

This will include your attitudes and beliefs towards success, leadership and money. Go back to the lists on pages 189 and 193, as well as choosing your own words. Look at the family you grew up in to see what you might have learned. Build up an holistic picture. When you are aware of the patterns holding you back, choose which areas have the highest level of emotional charge. They are the ones you need first to discharge so you can change the energy you bring to life and the energy you attract to yourself.

Next, *express* what has been building up inside of you. This may be cathartic and involve physical movement, or it may be through talking or writing. Build a healthy boundary between the pattern or behaviour and yourself.

Third, if you have made mistakes or hurt others, get in touch with what you need to clean up from the past. *Forgive* yourself and others for what has been done before so that you can move in with a fresh slate.

Finally, what *New Behaviour* might you put into practice? Does it involve a change of career completely, a change of job, or just different working habits? It could mean that you are communicating to your co-workers in a different way, or simplifying your life by cutting down your work hours. It could be that you commit to not bringing work home, or ending the pattern of perfectionism so that when something is done, you too can know it's done. As a potential leader, perhaps you go on courses to learn how to delegate and make strategy. If money has been a big issue, that is where you start to make changes.

Use the visioning technique on page 198 to see what it is that you would most like to do on all four levels of your being. By doing this, you are tapping into your own potential as well as going beyond the normal confines of the mind. You can also use the imaginary funeral visualisation to focus on a mission for your life. With this perspective about what really matters at the end of your life, you will have the courage to make an effective change in the present day.

Once you are clear about what is stopping you *and* what you want in your working life, you can be free to choose the occupation that you most desire. Start by acting on it today. There will be no holding you back.

12

Getting Beyond
Compulsive Patterns

The people who are the least addictive are those who are most
fulfilled spiritually and emotionally.

JOHN MARTIN

A lifestyle that depends on 'being out of it', is far more wide-spread than we believe. It is not only addicts who need distractions. In our fast-paced society, many of us are chasing money and power, fuelled by high-octane caffeine, tuned up by sugar, with alcohol there to take the lid off in the evening or weekend. Our spare time is often spent watching TV, surfing the Internet or just plain old-fashioned shopping. Society itself, in the phrase of Anne Wilson Schaef, has become an addict. How has this come about? What are we avoiding? Why is it so much easier to spend an evening in front of the TV with wine or a beer to hand than it is to talk with our loved ones?

If you look at your own behaviour, and this is by no means a comfortable task, are there things that you repetitively do that interfere with your own connection with yourself? Are you for example, always busy, continually filling your time up with one activity or another? There's even a word for you – 'busy-aholic'! If so, do you justify your busyness by saying that you have no choice? Do you feel you have a good balance between work and play, or between time at the office and time at home? Are your perhaps a perfectionist, so that whatever you do, it's never quite good enough? Do you absolutely have to be back for that particular TV programme, and God help anyone who gets in your way? Has food become very important to you? What about your relationships? Do you live your life around someone else and have become co-dependent?

What in your life might be a compulsion that is covering up what's truly going on? What do you do to distract yourself from yourself? This chapter will look at the patterns that have become our compulsive lifestyles and ways to break through them.

A tale of two brothers

I was the good boy at school. I did not smoke nor drink, and continuously received good reports from my teachers. I worked so hard at all my subjects that I never noticed people making friends and doing all those other normal things around me. Later, to make up for my lost youth, I got my highs by falling in love with a new woman roughly every three weeks. Though I was not tempted by drugs or drink, I was as hopeless at being with myself as was my brother.

My brother Justin was the bad boy. At school he started smoking hash and dropping the occasional tab of acid. He hardly passed one exam and was the bane of all the teachers. He had a wide circle of friends who he kept in touch with after school. When he started working, he moved on to coke, heroin and designer drugs – whatever he could find to change his mood. He lost various jobs because of his unreliability and would soon find new ones because of his charm. He was given to excess, always doing more drugs than anyone else. Eventually he had either been fired from or walked out of every job, and every friendship he made had at one point been tested beyond the breaking point. Everything he had followed had led to a dead end, and he felt himself a complete failure.

The strange thing was that we were *both* living an addict's lifestyle, compulsively acting out to avoid an uncomfortable reality – ourselves. He depended on drugs, I depended on work, sex and love. His way was through substances, mine was through behaviours. Being compulsive is very widespread. Who do you know who behaves like an addict?

Deep down, we sense an emptiness. We are all trying to fill that old inner void in whatever way we can.

WE TALK LIKE ADDICTS

If society itself really is an addict, then we not only act but also talk like addicts. We've all heard those phrases from others and probably used them ourselves. They are the favourites which excuse our compulsive behaviour: *I can give smoking up any time I want; I only do it because I'm bored; I have to exercise for hours a day otherwise I can't sleep at night; one more chocolate bar isn't going to make any difference; I only drink a glass or two to relax; this time I KNOW he's the one; I'm going to give up next week – honest; I only watch soap operas because there's nothing else on* . . . It's the 'just once more won't do any harm' syndrome. The language of addiction is steeped in denial, and a refusal to face what is happening in the moment. Addiction and denial go hand in hand and make for a powerful alliance.

There's nothing wrong with me, OK?

According to the dictionary, the main definition of denial is the 'disbelief in the existence or the reality of a thing; a refusal to recognise or acknowledge, a disowning or disavowal.' This, in layman's terms, translates into 'there's nothing wrong with me'. *I need a drink to get up in the morning/I can't get through the day without my packet of cigarettes/I have to take my mobile to the bathroom otherwise I might miss a call/I just need to clean up some more/I have to have one hit off this joint before I can relax/everyone else but me has a problem*, and so on . . . *What's more I don't need to change, and if you don't like how I am, well, that's your problem.*

So what's underneath?

People who have at one time been addicts often say that they have given up the anaesthetic that was covering up the pain, but of course the pain – of feeling isolated, or different, anxious or depressed, is still there. To heal themselves, they need fully to contact the pain that caused them to reach for that way of dulling their feelings originally. They must feel it again in order to come through it to the other side. The other side is a place of integral goodness, a place where they can feel fine just as they are. This is true for all of us who run around compulsively.

Beneath any compulsive behaviour pattern or addiction, from seemingly innocuous ones like watching TV to more serious drug habits, the same cry can be heard. When we stop long enough to listen we can hear it. It's the voice of a sad, lonely person crying, 'Please love me' (the core pattern could be called 'feeling abandoned'). Buried deep inside each of us with an addiction is the voice of our childlike Emotional self crying out in pain, asking to be loved, just as we asked our parents when we were children. It is no longer conscious and many of us actively in addiction may never stop and listen. But until we stop and learn to take responsibility for our inner healing, we go on trying to fill the gaping hole within us. We'll try anything we can to get away from the pain and toxic shame of there being something fundamentally wrong with us. *What kind of person must I be for this to happen to me? I know, I'll escape from this by smoking, drinking, drug-taking, being self-righteous, gambling, and so on.*

We desperately wish to avoid feeling pain. Our favourite compulsions are the ways we know that 'work best'.

Pia Mellody, an addiction expert, says that an addiction is 'any process which removes an intolerable reality'. Any kind of addictive substances, activities or behaviours can be mood-changers. We need them to numb out how we are really feeling about ourselves, to make us feel better, to give us the courage to don that 'I'm fine mask' and go out and face the world. Bob Hoffman called it 'putting whipped cream on the garbage'. The problem is that after the effect has worn off, we're still feeling the same and probably worse because we *know* in our heart of hearts that what we are doing to ourselves is not only highly destructive but also adding to our toxic shame. We can't bear to feel that sense of being wrong or not good enough just as we are. To escape from it we indulge in our addictions, and the vicious cycle continues.

I'm not good enough
*There's something
wrong with me to do
this to myself*

addictive behaviour
*of some kind to
escape the pain*

provides the quick fix
*Ah, that feels better!
But not for long*

self hate
*Why do I do this
to myself?*

The vicious cycle of addictive behaviour

We end up acting out our addictions and completely relying on them in order to function. After a while our addictions, whether an actual substance or a behaviour, have taken such a compulsive hold over our lives that we forget why we started them in the first place. However, it is always our emotional patterns that drive us into some kind of addiction. See the pathways to alcoholism in the box below.

THE PATHWAYS TO ALCOHOLISM

Certain emotional patterns seem to make people more likely to find emotional relief in one substance rather than another. For example, there are two emotional pathways to alcoholism. One starts with someone who was high-strung and anxious back in childhood, who typically discovers as a teenager that alcohol will calm anxiety. Very often they are children – usually sons – of alcoholics who themselves have turned to alcohol to soothe their nerves. The second emotional pathway to alcoholism comes from a high level of agitation, impulsivity and boredom. This pattern shows up in infancy as being restless, cranky and hard to handle, in grade school as having the 'fidgets', hyperactivity and getting into trouble, a propensity that, as we have seen, can push such children to seek out friends on the fringe – sometimes leading to a criminal career or the diagnosis of antisocial personality disorder.

Daniel Goleman, *Emotional Intelligence*

HOW DO WE GET SO HOOKED?

Addictions carry false promises because they give us hope that they will make us feel better: 'I will make you feel good; I will stop you feeling sad or lonely.' It's easy to understand if it's a substance. Certainly, when we first start to smoke, or take a hit, or use anything which creates that initial quick fix-it buzz, something happens to make us feel better because it alters the chemicals in our brain. With most of these substances, our mood is heightened. Of course, those euphoric feelings wear off just as rapidly with the result that the 'rush' becomes a memory. We try to get back to that feeling by continuing to use the addiction. But each time we need more and more to get the same buzz, and before long we're hooked.

All compulsions are a variation on this cycle of needing more to block the feelings underneath. This includes society's current favourite, caffeine, with its dealer on every corner promising to make the day more zesty and enjoyable.

The compulsion behind a behaviour is less easy to understand, but no less addictive. How can people get addicted to TV, you wonder? Well, it so numbs the brain that we might as well be on Valium. Apparently TV requires less concentration than is needed to choose which vegetable to eat during a meal. Exercise produces endorphins, short for endogenous, or the body's own, morphine. Sex and romance produce a veritable cocktail of chemicals, including dopamine, oxytocin and pheromones. If the romance isn't going so well, there's always chocolate to gorge on. There are a lot of natural and legal substances to get addicted to.

Mind sets can also be compulsive

Jackie had been suffering from depression for over twenty-five years. To escape it, she jumped into any relationship she could find. Only thing was, as soon as her depression surfaced, she became too much for the other person to bear, and the relationship would eventually break down. Of course this made her more depressed and would start once more the search for a new relationship.

She followed a visualisation where she was given the opportunity to feel completely and consciously every aspect of her depression as an addiction. When Jackie indulged in it with her full attention, she clearly saw the depression itself as a repeating pattern. Jackie started imagining bringing golden light into the dark and empty space she had always felt inside. She consciously worked on building a new relationship with herself, founded on self-forgiveness and love.

Jackie is now able to recognise depression coming a

long way off. She is also much more aware of its effect on her. Now, instead of subconsciously asking to be surrounded by the old, familiar and comforting dark cloud of misery, she sees another way of responding. She gives herself the chance of living with a much more positive energy around her. She welcomes life rather than pushes it away.

Jackie's compulsive behaviour did not involve a substance or even an activity. Hers was the recurrent mind-set of depression. She became addicted to depression because it provided an easy route out of facing reality.

Depressed people sometimes justify this kind of rumination by saying they are trying to 'understand themselves better'. In fact they are priming the feelings of sadness without taking any steps that might actually lift their mood . . . a passive immersion in the sadness simply makes it worse.

Daniel Goleman

Anxiety can have the same result. Free-floating worry creates a comforting stream of adrenaline. Strangely, this makes us feel more engaged with our lives. Adrenaline is said to be more addictive than nicotine. Other mind-sets to watch out for on the compulsive level are perfectionism and self-righteousness. Perfectionism is the perpetual inner nag that tells us to keep going. Self-righteousness compensates well for life's ups and downs. It's other name is being smug.

Whether it's through substances or behaviours, we are using something to avoid the uncomfortable reality of our lives.

LOOKING FOR A
SPIRITUAL CONNECTION

For most of us 'normally neurotic' members of society, neurosis is fundamentally the state of feeling unlovable. Not that we *are* unlovable, but the fact that we feel that way is a result of the lack of love we have for ourselves. Just as the Hoffman Process is based on the spiritual principles of connecting us back to a source of love both within and without, so we work with addictive substances and behaviours. They are seen not as a physical or intellectual, and not even as an emotional disease, but fundamentally as a *spiritual* disease. Disconnected from our own spiritual nature, we reach out for a substance or activity to fill that ghastly sense of emptiness. If only we could remember that, rather than being empty, we are connected to a source of endless love.

One day Bob Hoffman had a spiritual awakening, just as Bill W. and Dr Bob, the co-founders of Alcoholics Anonymous, did. They all woke up to seeing clearly the need to restore themselves to a healthy sense of balance with themselves as well as a higher form of power or guidance. Their teachings share many aspects, such as the step of taking a full inventory of our behaviour (which we call 'patterns') and the need to forgive and ask for forgiveness. They also stressed that life is an ongoing process of taking daily inventory and admitting we can still make mistakes. Both systems are powerful tools for self-realisation. They should be used consciously with self-love, and not as internal tyrants telling us what we are still doing wrong. The two systems also agree that our own development will be more grounded if we pass on what we have learned to others.

How Do We Conquer Addictions?

To conquer your addiction you first have to ask yourself, 'Am I prepared to give up this substance or this behaviour for good?' It's no good half-heartedly saying, 'Oh well, I'll give it a shot for the next few hours.' That way you pull the wool over your own eyes, looking for a way out of the discomfort through the back door. Breaking addictive habits is challenging: you have to get real with yourself and take full responsibility for who you are and what you create in your life. As Steven Covey, author of *The Seven Habits of Highly Effective People*, says: 'You are responsible for your life. Decide what you should do and get on with it. The ability to subordinate an impulse to a value is the essence of the proactive person.'

Imagine waking up with a feeling of contentment spreading throughout your body and having that feeling increase through the day. You might even call it self-love. What if you went through life driven by self-love rather than feeling at times empty, depressed and unsatisfied? It certainly would take the edge off the need to drown yourself in work or drink, food or daytime TV.

The way forward is to replace your innermost feelings with self-love so that you can live fully from your own values, and therefore free of any dependence on substances or behaviours. This is no magic cure. It takes enormous self-discipline, skilful use of techniques and ritual.

Ritual, you may remember, is one of the three pillars, along with therapy and education, that underpin this process of change. Ritual encourages you to separate from your normal reality for a while in order to confront a part of, and gain a deeper understanding of, yourself. Having done that, you then return back to reality, bringing along your new-found wisdom. Much of the expressive work we have done is ritualistic, as was the part that moves us into forgiveness. When you journey deep into an emotion to explore it, you separate yourself from the world, just as in a ritual. The many visualisations that we have been using to contact your Spiritual self or sanctuary are also rituals.

You have learned to use these rituals yourself. Now, a simple visualisation can safely take you into the core of your addictive personality. This is the modern-day 'dragon' we all have to slay. You can give yourself the opportunity really to sense and to see what you are doing to yourself, and feel safe doing so. With this heightened awareness, you can then reach beyond the addictive personality, which is not your real self anyway, but a false mask you put on to make life more bearable. You can reach into and touch the authentic nature of your Spiritual self, the part of you free of self destruction and, just as importantly, of self judgement. In this way, you actually experience that state of being within you which is completely at peace and unconditionally accepting of what is. You climb out of the 'comfortably numb' armchair that addictive behaviour creates for you. The change that people undergo having experienced this connection with the higher aspect of themselves is often very inspiring.

A RITUALISED VISUALISATION TO HELP BREAK ADDICTIONS

To benefit fully from this exercise, give yourself some time, around 15 or 20 minutes, when you will not be disturbed. Settle into a comfortable position and centre yourself by focusing on your breathing for a couple of minutes. If possible, suggest that a friend record this onto a tape for you with some quiet music in the background. If you are reading it to yourself, pause to allow the images to impact your mind.

Imagine you are in a prison of your own addictions. There are walls around you and no windows. It feels very dark and hopeless. You feel you have no choice left in life, and you are tired, very tired. However, one thing keeps you alive with a sense of hope. It's the knowledge deep within that you still possess some free will. Armed with that glimmer of hope, you *choose* to find a way to be free.

In that prison, you start feeling around in the darkness for the hidden handle of a trap door. Allow yourself to take it in both your hands and then, with a deep breath, lift it up and feel yourself floating out of the prison into a beautiful spot in nature. It could be a favourite meadow, beach or forest glade. This is your sanctuary, a place in which you feel completely safe. Look around you and feel the freshness of the air and how a light warm breeze touches your face. How does that feel? Let yourself feel the pleasant sensations in your body as you gently breathe.

Now become connected with your Spiritual self by touching your heart and forming an image of your idealised self. It's your face, washed clear of any concerns, radiating peace and tranquillity. Breathe into that spot, allowing it to transmit white light to all parts of your being. Stay for a few moments with that sense of connectedness to yourself. Now imagine you are being lifted up a magic stairway into pure light, far, far above you. You are rising, leaving behind any earthly worries you may have. In the light, breathe and feel completely welcomed and at home. You are back home at the place you feel most comfortable.

After a few minutes, ask your Spiritual self to go back down to that prison and bring back a supply of drink, drugs, junk food, or whatever it is that you have been

addicted to. If it's a behaviour such as gambling, relationships or work, keep it in mind. Come back to the light
with it and really indulge in it. Let yourself fully go – have
a binge, overdo it. Drink, smoke, overeat, imagine
watching hour upon hour of TV, mindlessly work on a
computer, read and read, load yourself up with new
clothes, have mindless sex. Then, after a few minutes, stop
and feel what has happened to your body and your
connection with your own Spiritual self. Check in also
with how removed you now probably feel. Remember this
feeling, this living hell and stay with it for a few moments.

Now make a choice. Imagine there is a crossroads in
front of you. To the left lies the path you have known and
always taken, one where you give in to your impulses of
self-destructiveness. See yourself walking down that left
road, indulging in another few years of those addictions.
You are even more worn-out and more deeply depressed.
Let yourself feel the pointlessness of going on that way.
Stay there a couple of minutes, and then return to the
crossroads.

To the right lies another way – the way where you are
led by your Spiritual self. This will mean giving up your
old ways and your daily 'anaesthetics'. But by giving those
up, you get yourself back in a much more authentic way.
As with all things, you have to give something up to find
place for a new reality to step in. See yourself walking
down this right road, feeling calm and peaceful and full
of self-love. Think of how different your life would be in
all areas if you chose this way. Stay on this road for a
couple of minutes, and then return to the crossroads.

This is your choice: to take the left road, the one you
know, or a new direction, where you give up your usual

control and allow yourself to be led by your Spiritual self. What do you want to do? If it is difficult to decide, remember that sitting on the fence is also a decision. Jump off the fence and let yourself live in a different way.

If you decide to take the right road, then continue with this exercise. If you do not, then know that your choice is also valid. Do not force yourself before you are ready.

Once you have surrendered to your Spiritual self, and taken the right road, then allow yourself to reconnect with the power of the light. Kneel down and be forgiven by the light, or Higher Power, and know that you have never been rejected by the light. It may have been you in the past who rejected it, but now it is yours to re-connect with at any time you feel like. Breathe it in and allow yourself to fully feel what that does to your being. When you are ready, come back and open your eyes.

Feel yourself fully back in your body and take note of any insights you had. To give them even more force, write down those insights, or goals, or commitments that you made.

THE BODY SCAN

To help addictions it is essential that we become consciously aware of them, and see ourselves as bigger than they are. This is another, shorter technique that can also be very helpful:

When a craving hits, stop what you are doing and bring your full attention to it. Then, instead of reaching for a cigarette, bar of chocolate, cream cake or whatever your current passion is, close your eyes and scan your body in your mind's eye, with your palm facing you.

Ask your inner wisdom where the craving is hiding in your body. It could be in your head, deep in your chest, or held in your solar plexus. It's very much your own personal experience and perception. Once you have located it, place your hand over the area, and breathe. Now talk to the craving and feel it fully. If you find it difficult to sense, turn it into a colour or shape. The important thing is first to make a connection with it, so then you can become more powerful than it. Just by becoming consciously aware of it helps to break its vice-like grip. Then you can breathe into this area and feel it softening. Breathing out, let it go from you. You can repeat this exercise any time you feel an addictive urge.

The peaceful spot

One way to break a substance addiction, once you are aware of it, is to remove yourself, together with the substance, to a quiet place away from other people. As you feel the urge, consciously ask yourself if you *really* need that cigarette or cup of coffee or bar of chocolate, etc. Look at it, study it, allow yourself to feel the discomfort, and above all *forgive* yourself. Doing this mindfulness meditation will alone help ease the grip of your addiction. If you still feel a compulsion to indulge, do so with compassion for the emptiness that you have lived with for years. Make a promise to yourself to continue on the healing process.

Emotions and Intellect working together

Remember the exercises we have done to create more harmony between your emotions and your intellect? This is one area where it is really worthwhile investigating what is going on within our own minds.

If you could hear the argument in your head every time you craved something, what would it sound like? 'Oh no, I really shouldn't.' 'Just one more, come on.' 'I'm only doing this so I can get on with things.' 'Oh well, everyone else is.'

Listening deeper, what do we find going on? As we know, buried beneath layers of old pain is the voice of a child crying out for love and attention. But now we're grown up, our Intellect is tired of listening to the moaning and complaining. These days we're busy, we have many pressures to attend to, so rather than attending to the needs of our childish Emotional self, we reach for the remedy to make things roll on smoothly. 'What we all need is a stiff drink' is what I heard when anything like a feeling started to emerge in my family. 'I think I'll just zonk out in front of a trashy movie,' we say after a busy day. Again and again, we don't pay attention to our emotional needs. But we pay for it . . . The chatter might sound something like this:

Emotional self: I need some time to feel

Intellect: Trouble is, you feel too much, and it gets in my way.

Emotional self: Well then, I'm going to make your life really difficult

Intellect: Oh no, you won't.

Emotional self: I'm so bored and depressed. Nothing exciting ever happens.

Intellect: (going back to the computer screen). Shut up, will you, I'm trying to work here. You'll get a couple of drinks this evening.

Emotional self: (seeing a woman passing by) Oh look, there's someone who may look after me better. Hmmm, I'd love a relationship with her.

You probably know by now how to fill in the rest of the story! If a relationship doesn't fit your emotional needs, you could substitute comfort eating, helping others, shopping. For the Intellect, the addiction here is work. It could just as easily be the behaviours of having to be the best or having to be right.

Before you indulge in your automatic, compulsive reaction, stop yourself. In that moment, check in first with your Emotional self. Ask yourself what you are feeling, and if there are any needs that are getting ignored. If you are not rushed for time, look back at the exercise that Brooke did in Chapter Seven (see page 103), where she takes the position of her Emotional self and proclaims her needs. Then turn it around and listen to what the Intellect has to say. Back and forth, back and forth they each go until they have said all they need to say. At that point they can sit down and draw up a truce between them.

By listening in, you are developing a sense of harmony between the emotions and the intellect. This harmony or truce allows you to go a long way down that path towards healing old habits. As the two selves stop fighting with each other, the destructive chatter ceases in your head, and you are able to become much more present in your life and trusting in your own process of healing.

An internal battle

A painter called David had smoked since he was fifteen. 'I'm so tired of this never-ending battle,' he told me one day. 'One part of me wants to give up smoking, but the other part of me can't. No, not true. It *won't*. It's driving me mad. Every morning I get up and promise myself that today is it. Today I'm giving up. And every day by nine o'clock there I am puffing away again.'

I asked him what were the reasons he smoked.

'Well, let's see. To calm my nerves. For inspiration. To take a break. Because it's the one thing that I enjoy. Because it's "against the rules". Because all the cool rebels smoke. Because it helps me keep thin.'

Broadly, those looked like the emotional response. What about the adult response?

'It's a disgusting habit. It's anti-social. It's a waste of money. Everyone disapproves. It's really bad for my health.'

No wonder there was a conflict inside. David had to do some work to resolve the feelings of his Emotional self before he could give up. Firstly, to heighten his awareness, I asked him to note down whenever he wanted a smoke. Then I had him smoke alone and not do anything else at the time. No chatting, no reading, no eating, no TV. He had to make the cigarette his meditation. If it didn't kill his enjoyment, I calculated, it would at least make him much more aware of his feelings at the time. He began to see that he needed a cigarette whenever he felt slightly nervous or socially awkward. It was a prop.

'So how old does that awkward part of you feel?' I asked in a session.

'About nine or ten', he said.

I had him imagine talking to that part of him, the child who had always felt awkward. 'Let him know that you understand his feelings. Ask him what you might do instead.'

His instinctive response was that he needed to fill out his social life. He was already a great cook so he decided to throw regular dinner parties in his home. When I saw him a few months later, he was not only not smoking, but said that he did not even feel the urge anymore.

A LASTING PEACE

When you are able to quiet the conflicts of your mind, you can stop and just listen. The basis of all spiritual traditions is to return to that silence and in that silence contact a higher wisdom. In the model of the Quadrinity, now is the time when you can contact the 'still, small voice within' of the Spiritual self. You can listen to your own inner truth and uncover the loving truth that you are your own best teacher and source of wisdom, after all.

Staying in contact with your Spiritual self also means that you are drinking from a bottomless cup of love. The power that this gives you is much stronger than that of your old habits. With that sense of inner fulfilment, you can lead a life free of compulsive behaviour. You no longer need to distract yourself from reality. You will have harnessed the power to get what you truly want from life.

13

Spirits in a Material World

Can't you see me standing before you cloaked in stillness?

RAINER MARIA RILKE

Once you have cleared yourself of old issues by moving through the stages of the Process, the key to building into your life new, positive ways of being and acting is simple. Be guided by your Spiritual self. With your Spiritual self in the lead you are listening to a voice of wisdom and love that is replenished by a universal, divine energy.

However, your connection with your sense of a higher, or Spiritual, self within you may not be as strong as you would like it to be. Guidance from your Spiritual self may be drowned out by noisy chatter from the other aspects of your being. You probably feel that there is never enough time to develop your spirituality. It somehow does not find much of a place in your busy life. What with the thousand and one things that needed to be fitted into each day, *and* needing to sleep, spirituality feels like a luxury. You tell yourself that you would have to be retired or drop out completely to make time for that side of life.

Of course there are practical reasons for not being able to make your spiritual connection a priority. But are you prepared to look beyond that, though, to see if that is the whole truth?

SPIRITUALITY AND RELIGION

What do you personally feel is the difference between spirituality and religion? Many of us are forced to accept a certain religion as children. We are not allowed to question it. 'Faith' means trusting that your parents always know what is best for you, and in this case it is their own religion. Some of us were brought up associating our religion with guilt and suffering. As we grow older, and start to question that religion, it seems to fall far short of what we would want naturally for a spiritual connection. Consequently some have turned their backs on anything remotely connected to spiritual understanding. They miss out on something which is not only precious and beautiful but also vital for everyone's personal development.

A spiritual connection is not specific to any religion. But any religion can provide the link and the practices to feel that connection again. After all, '*re-ligio*' means 'to relink'.

Patterns around spirituality

If you have had a deep religious conditioning that you feel is no longer serving your own truth, you might need to undo it. You might have to separate the messages that fill you with fear and guilt from the ones that inspire you. A parallel is often made between the God that a family invokes and their own style of parenting. So for some, God is a punishing figure who is ready to chastise you whenever you do or say 'the wrong thing'. The punishment block that awaits you when you die is called Hell. In other families, God is a benevolent, kindly figure who dispenses wisdom and kindness. At the end of life Heaven awaits. Which kind of God were you introduced to as a child?

Many people now have thrown 'the baby out with the bath-water' and no longer attend a church or even know others who do. But almost everyone I know still yearns for a spiritual connection. They are looking for it all the time, whether they pray, meditate, surf, write poetry, ride motorbikes, study cloud formations or walk the dog.

If something is holding you back, work on the patterns that interfere with your own spiritual connection. Become aware of what is in the way and put a name to it. For example, the patterns might be 'cynicism', 'I don't have the time' or 'what's the point?'

Just as there are patterns around money, leadership and success, there are specific patterns we have picked up over the years about religion and spirituality. If we were made to go to church and sit through hours of sermons, the pattern that comes up now would probably be 'It's too boring'. We might have been forced at an early age to learn texts by rote from a holy book rather than discover them through our own efforts. Even though these words may have been full of wonderful poetry, their innate beauty is coloured by the very fact that we did not have a choice about when and how to read them. If we heard our parents preaching, 'Love your neighbour as your-self' and then saw them shouting at the neighbours, our minds would have seen religion as meaningless or hypocritical. The word of God might only have operated on Sundays in some families. The rest of the week is devoid of spiritual or religious connection. It becomes a special day at a special place, rather than integrated in our lives.

We cannot wait until we're old enough not to have to go to the church or synagogue. The problem is, we never replace it, and lose a sense of ritually honouring that connection.

On the other hand, we might have grown up in a family that never went to church or kept a sense of the sacred aspect of life. If that was the case, spirituality would have been discounted either explicitly by phrases such as 'You can't prove it' or implicitly by attaching no importance to it whatsoever. Have you similarly discounted its importance?

When you discover patterns, make a list of them. Then, get in touch with how they may have limited you or even harmed you. Express the frustrations you have felt with those patterns through writing or by using your voice. Don't let the old charge fester away in you causing bitterness.

Next, understand that the people who may have taught you those patterns were also conditioned. If it was a priest or a minister who taught you, or even hurt you, bring them into the picture. Acknowledge that what they did to you was a result of their own programming. They were also being human and as humans we are all prone to interpreting a spiritual message in a limited way. Which is why it is said that we are all human, all too human. It is also said that to err is human, but to forgive is divine. Forgive them for what they did so that you can move on and create a new practice and belief in your own true spirituality.

BUILDING A SPIRITUAL PRACTICE

There are various ways with which to regain a strong sense of spiritual connection. The first is through being more conscious of one fact. Remember the fundamental truth that we are spiritual beings having a human experience. That way, we can get things in perspective. If we thought of ourselves as human beings having a spiritual experience, we would only expect the occasional moment of peace and transcendence. Thinking of ourselves as spirit existing in a human world makes us see this life as a continual unfolding and learning. All we have to remember is to come back to our higher natures.

The second way is a more practical one. We sometimes think we have to go off to a monastery to feel our spiritual nature. We believe we might have to renounce the world to be in touch with the sacred. But we can stay in touch very simply, through a daily check-in. Just as we check in with our thoughts and feelings, and with our body, we can remember to check in on a spiritual level. We can do that very simply through the breath.

Our word 'spirit' derives from the Latin for 'breath'. Many traditions around the world focus on the breath as a link to the divine. In the Latin-derived languages such as French, Italian and Portuguese, to 'inspire' means to breathe in. To 'expire' means to breathe out. It gives a refreshing outlook if we consider that at every moment we are both inspiring and expiring! So, on a practical level, use breathing to remember your spirit inside.

Breathing has other benefits. Being more conscious of it calms and centres you. Indeed, it is used as the focus of the Buddhist practice called Vipassana, or 'insight meditation'. Here you are taught to bring a very fine awareness to your breathing. Try it – feel your breath as it goes through your nostrils or makes your abdomen rise and fall. Do you sense the gap in time between the in breath and the out breath? If so, you have had a moment of pure awareness, beyond mind.

The third way is through the powers of imagination. At various times throughout the day *see* yourself as a spirit being in human form. Remember the exercises we did in Chapter Three? This is better done with eyes closed. If you have already recorded one or two visualisations, add it to your tape. Or ask a friend to read it out to you.

SEEING YOUR SPIRITUAL SELF

Imagine your own face, cleared of worries. The expression on your face radiates quiet power, wisdom and love. That's you, and you are a spiritual being. You have taken on human form. Yes, your programmed self may have patterns that fall short of purity and clarity, but you the Spiritual self can show them another way. You are leading the way down that right road towards freedom, love and serenity. Remember the essential being behind the human form. It's you, the 'I am that I am'.

For added power, imagine yourself back in the sanctuary of the mind you created back in Chapter Three. Go into the light for an infusion of pure loving energy whenever you feel a lack, or a loss of connection.

Make your life more simple! Over thousands of years, man has left the busy-ness of the world behind to connect with himself and something far greater than himself. It's no coincidence that at least three major religions originated in the desert. In silence is heard the voice of the eternal. In the wide open space the sense of the infinite, and man's small part, can be felt. To regain our true nature, we must aim for more simplicity and less activity. What *doing* can you give up in your life? You could replace some of the doing with simply being, instead. Do you have too much stuff? Throw it out and take some space back for your being-ness.

Daily, there are bound to be times when you feel more connected to yourself and to others. How can you best reinforce that? What are some of the practical steps you can take?

Think of the *situations* where you feel connected to the greater whole. Does that happen when you are by yourself, or with others? Are you inside or in nature? Build those situations into your daily or weekly routine. Then think of the *times* when you feel connected. Are there certain times of day? For me, the early morning is the best time, or when I'm doing something physical. Knowing that, I bring more awareness to those times and situations. I still have to make an effort to remember my spiritual nature. I wish the awareness was simply there, but after many years, many books and many Masters, I need reinforcement! I need to hear that my Spiritual self also has a voice.

SENSING YOUR SPIRITUAL SELF

Here's a longer meditation you can use to bring forth your spirit which focuses on the breath. Allow yourself at least ten minutes for this. Put it on a tape if you wish.

Get in touch with the rhythm of your breathing. Imagine as you breathe that you are taking breath in to the centre of your being. Take a long, gentle breath to relax your body, letting out a gentle sigh as you breathe out. Take a long, gentle breath to relax your mind, letting out a gentle sigh as you breathe out. Take a long, gentle breath to relax your emotions, letting out a gentle sigh as you breathe out.

Dropping into a space of deep relaxation, imagine that instead of air you are breathing light into your body. Bring it especially into your heart. Feel yourself being filled with light and with love.

You are breathing the energy of life, of power, of love. This is your energy, your power, your love. You are filled and bathed by the light. This light is your essence, your

Spiritual self. This breath is your very life, yours to take and release, yours to give and to receive. This is the energy of your spiritual self here for you in every moment. This is your essence, at the core of your being, your power and your wisdom. This is your Spiritual self that has been within you your entire life. That is always present. That has bought you to healing. That has brought you goodness. Your essence that is wisdom, that is love.

Feel the light around you emanating from your light, connecting you with the universal light, giving and receiving. Experience the abundance of light and of love.

Now use these words, or similar ones, to give voice to the spirit inside:

I, the Spiritual self, I am that I am.
I am our essence.
I am our wisdom and our creativity.
I am our voice and our guide for eternity.
I create our loving vision.
I lead us on the path of love.
I believe in our positive future.
I know our true potential.
I am at one, I am connected to the universe.

I am you and you are me.
We are all parts of the whole.

When you feel the connection with yourself, keep that soft focus, and come back to your current reality.

Possible objections in your adult life

It's not only patterns from the past that can stop you having a powerful spiritual practice. The main objection may be still within you. How are the other three parts of your Quadrinity doing while you attempt these visualisations and meditations? It's always better to hear their possible objections rather than push them under the blanket. Mine go something like this after a few minutes sitting quietly.

Emotional self: This is so boring! Is anything going to happen, or are we just going to sit here, doing absolutely nothing?

Intellect: I don't know about you, but I've got a lot of things on my plate right now. I can think of better ways to be spending my time rather than sitting around looking holy.

Emotional self: Looking holy? I think we probably look really silly. I hope no one walks in. I'd be really embarrassed.

Intellect: If this made any sense, I might be able to go along with it. But I can't see any possible benefits. Besides, we'd be better off reading about spirituality.

Emotional self: There must be something I can do that's more fun than this. Isn't there meant to be a good film around these days?

Body: Will the two of you stop chattering away! I'm trying to get comfortable here, and you're giving me a headache. Besides, trying to sit still hurts my knees. On top of which, my back is sore and I'm hungry.

Emotional self: Hungry? Hmm, I wonder if there's any of that chocolate left over. Let's go find out . . .

Make sure that these three are well set up to meditate or have some quiet time. That means that your body is reasonably comfortable and is not going to sabotage you straightaway. If your Intellect needs reassurance on the rational level, satisfy it by looking up research on the benefits of meditation. Herbert Benson's *The Relaxation Response* is the classic on that subject. Emotionally, if there is an issue that is very much to the forefront, you may need to deal with it and then meditate. As your meditation practice deepens, however, you can simply observe the emotions as another aspect of experience, without being hijacked by them.

CONNECTED TO OTHERS

You are not alone. You may not always realise this as you travel alone, or live alone, or hunger for a relationship. But we are all connected both by the air we breathe – the spirit, or breath – and by the love that is given to us as a divine gift. Knowing that makes our daily life full of possible spiritual connection. When you meet someone, look at them and remind yourself that they also have a wonderful Spiritual self. That means even, or especially, if their patterns are bothering you at the time!

SENSING A UNIVERSAL CONNECTION

You can use a short meditation to remind yourself of this connection to all others in this world of ours. This heals the sense of separation that has caused so much unhappiness. Choose some quiet background music to heighten the experience.

As you breathe, feel that breath coming from your core essence. Feel it filling you, and nurturing you. Imagine the breath as light. See it as your inner light growing brighter and stronger, filling and surrounding all parts of you as you acknowledge your own power and wisdom and love.

Experience the joy that this light brings to you, to all aspects of your mind, and to your body. You have so much to give because you are part of the endless source of love. The source of this light is also the source of all love.

As you breathe, feel that love expanding to touch the person you most love in the world. See it as a point of light reaching them and softening their heart. Then let that love, that light move out from one person to the others to whom you are most closely connected. Feel yourself sharing with them, giving to them, nourishing them from your essence. Then, experience yourself receiving love and light and nourishment from others in your life. Let yourself be fully open to the abundance.

Now that light, that love, that compassion from your open heart reaches out to embrace and touch the whole world. We are all beings as one, connected by the air we breathe and the love and light of the universe that we share: hearts opening together in this journey of life; spirits here on earth recognising the spirits of others; knowing that as we share the air around us, we remember, with every breath that we take, that we are all one, all connected. All of us find, in this connection, that life becomes simple. All we have to do is be. We are 'beings of love', giving and receiving, both for this life and for hereafter.

When you feel the connection with others, keeping that soft focus within, gently return yourself to the world you now live in.

Jeremy Davidson, a man who left the city to grow his own food and to live as simply as he can, told me that he uses his hand to connect with his sense of spirit. He will 'anchor' the feeling he has from a morning meditation in some part of his body. One day it might be in his heart area, another day in his abdomen. By putting his hand on that part of his body during the day, he says, he is instantly reminded of his true, deeper nature.

Where might *your* anchor be when you feel yourself drifting?

Spirituality in every moment

When you are open to life, you start noticing the divine in everything. God could be a child at play, the eyes of a lover, the touch of someone's skin, the singing of the birds, the sound of rain on the roof, the wind over the long grass. It could be in the smile of the person serving you a meal, the unexpected call from an old friend or the words in a conversation. God really is in the details.

Sometimes the details can be so rich that we need to keep a simple view of the bigger picture, though. If you were to remember just three things to help you build a stronger sense of your own true spirituality, then remember these:

- Make time every day
- Set aside a physical space
- Watch your breathing

You don't have to keep searching. What you are looking for is already right here, right now, within you.

14

Tune into Your Body

Sing, my tongue, of the mystery of the glorious body.

ST THOMAS AQUINAS

It's now time we turned to the fourth aspect of our Quadrinity, the body, so that we can bring harmony to all parts of our being. We often lose a sense of really being *in* our bodies, especially if we do a job that requires sitting down and processing thoughts and ideas all day. In a society that puts a high value on knowledge and information, the body can be easily disregarded.

Our body is our physical self, and we need to stay in touch with what it is we want as well as what our current attitudes are towards this important aspect.

Remember that the body does not just host the trillions of neurons that run our emotional and intellectual selves. It is also the home of our Spiritual self; it's our sacred spiritual home. The body is therefore as worthy of being heard and cared for as our Spiritual self. Like our spirit, it too gives and receives the flow of life's abundant energy. It has a vital part to play in the display of love. Indeed the body 'makes love'; it expresses love for another person physically through sex. It is our channel to that sensual, pleasurable and even sacred world of sex.

To keep a healthy relationship with our bodies, we need

234

from time to time to stop and take stock of what is happening with it. We need to check up on our own physical being.

It's everyone's goal to have a healthy mind in a healthy body. Feeling healthy and alive we give and receive pleasure; we can fully respond to life. It reflects the harmony between our thoughts and feelings. If that harmony is lost it quickly will let us know with a physical sign such as a headache or tiredness. We can even use it to attune to the moods and feelings of others. It's the channel to both what's going on inside and what's happening on the outside.

As the channel to the outside world, the body of course reflects our image, the important aspect, whether it's superficial or not, that we present to the world.

By turning our attention to it, we can learn much more from the inherent wisdom of the body. Then we can heal it if we need to and keep it attuned to what is best for it. Let's first look at the important connection between the body and the Spiritual self.

Treating our bodies as sacred

Carol was one of those people who you knew immediately really did *appreciate* her body. A former yoga teacher, she now designs and installs gardens. She works with her hands, is always outside and watches her diet without being too 'precious' about everything she eats. She and her girlfriends treat themselves to a day's treatment at a spa every two months. Her holidays are spent on gentle walks or cycling trips. Every year she spends a week on a retreat at a spiritual centre.

Sounds too good to be true, you say. I thought so, too, when I first met her. I watched carefully for the old wrappers of junk food to spill out from a pocket. Show me that you're normal! But she would not be caught out, because she was living this way without effort. It was simply her lifestyle, a style that made her feel best about herself. How did she do it?

Carol told me that the basis of treating her body well was her spiritual practice. When she had started meditating, she noticed how neglected her body was. Sitting quietly, putting attention on her breathing, she had an immediate 'in' to the current state of her physical being. Meditating daily has meant that she has stayed in touch with her body. If it is out of alignment and needs something, it lets her know quickly.

Honouring our bodies

Our Spiritual self, as we know, has taken on a human form, and lives in our body for our whole lifetime. We need to remember this. But, often we forget. Instead we consider our body as something that's simply there, demanding food and sleep, getting stiffer and older with every passing day. We live in a way that does not honour our bodies as the sacred home of our spiritual selves.

Do we consider every day, with awe, this miracle that makes us human? Without any conscious thought on our part, the hundreds of muscles move, the blood flows around, we process oxygen and food to provide energy and we regenerate billions of cells. We are born, learn to walk, run, dance, jump, celebrate life, make more babies and die with these bodies. It's time to fully appreciate what we have been given.

If you remember to appreciate the sacredness and miracle of your body, are you then ready to explore this aspect of your being more fully? How about looking at what is it that you want from your body?

BODY WISH LIST

If you could have it any way you wanted it, what would you consider to be a really good relationship with your body? What would you want more or less of? Would you give yourself more time to meditate and find stillness from the bustle of the day? Would your priority go towards being fit and having the right amount of body weight? Is it your wish to have a better posture? Would you look to practice and develop your own sense of movement and rhythm through dance? Would you simply wish to be *in* your body more in life? Would you want to have a more exciting sex life?

Fill in these phrases spontaneously. Don't let yourself think too much about them. It's your body talking, not your intellect!

- I'd like my body to be more . . .
- I'd like more of . . .
- I'd like less of . . .
- I'd like to spend more time with my body doing . . .

What did you find yourself wanting for your body? The next question is: how badly do you want it? If you want it enough, you're ready to do something about it.

Of course to get anywhere, we have to look at where we are now. So what's your relationship like with your body today?

YOUR BODY NOW

Consider how much of your attention goes towards your body. Right now, are you relaxed or tense? How are you sitting? How mindful of your posture are you? What did you have for your last meal? Was it nutritious and healthy? Was it prepared lovingly? How conscious were you of eating it? How is your breathing at this very moment – deep and even or shallow and fast?

Do you feel that you really nourish yourself with food? What type of food do you eat most regularly? Do you give your body regular exercise? Do you care for your 'instrument', as the great acting teacher Stanislavsky would call it?

How do you feel about your body? What is your own body image? On a scale of 0 to 10, with 10 being the highest score, how would you rate your body today?

NEGATIVE SELF-IMAGE

It's possible that you may not appreciate your body at all. If the image your hold of your body is negative, the first step is to acknowledge simply *that*. Then you can start to bring it out of a sense of hidden shame – and into the open. The voices that whisper can come out and be heard. Next you can address the reality of these voices and see if there is a need for change. Do you carry your own critic around with you?

Here are some of the most common areas of self-criticism. Tick them off mentally if they are true for you:

- [ ] I'm too fat
- [ ] I'm too thin
- [ ] I'm too old

- [ ] I'm too unfit
- [ ] I've got too many lines
- [ ] I've got too many spots
- [ ] I've got too much cellulite
- [ ] I eat too much junk food

If you find that you are your own worst critic, what is it that you do to change your body image? Do you say to yourself 'a new outfit will make me feel so much better' as you go marching off to the shopping mall with your credit card?

As you know very well, whatever you do to change your outside appearance will not make you feel better on the inside. The change has to come from within. So how can we really start to change our deep-set attitudes? As with other patterns that run our lives, we need to discover how we picked them up.

How we learned to love our bodies (or didn't)

We don't have to go far to see the messages that influence our own body image today. They bombard us in every film and TV show, are splashed across hundreds of billboards and fill thousands of pages of magazines. We end up believing, 'If I'm that thin, I'll feel really good. If I keep looking young I won't have any problems. That flat stomach will make me a more desirable mate. That perfume will attract a new lover. That dress will make me irresistible to my husband.'

We long to be attractive not for any sense of inner happiness, but so that we can be admired by someone else. That's in our supposedly adult world! In the older, childlike part of the mind, we wish for even more than that. We want to be *loved* by someone else. We feel we might just attract the love our heart still yearns for *if* we could only get the right look, clothes or even smell. Oh to be taller and thinner, we cry!

But long before we ever cast eyes on the idealised form of the first 'super model', we probably felt something lacking inside. Our bodies reflect what we feel is missing deep down – unconditional love. If we grew up with a lack of love as young beings, then we'll find it hard to love our bodies. And it will show.

Before the messages from the media and society, we were made vulnerable to negative images by our family background. This is why we need to go deep beneath the appearance to feel the inner truth.

If you *really* could have the 'perfect' body and 'beautiful' looks, how then would you feel about yourself? I expect in most cases, probably no different at all. Some of the most unhappy people I have met are physically strikingly beautiful. They shrink into their own secret pain because other people think they have everything going for them.

Crying inside

Gabrielle, a well-known actress, has had men throwing themselves at her feet all her life. After many short-term relationships, she developed Crohn's disease, brought on by worry and stress. There had been someone crying inside her all the time.

Gabrielle felt that as a child, she was not loved for who she was, but for what she looked like. She couldn't even relate to the pretty little girl with blonde curls and big blue eyes of whom her parents were so proud. Her mother wanted to know about every aspect of her life, but never ever simply held her and told her she was loved. She was put up as a contestant in child beauty pageants and later sent off to learn how to be a model. All this time she felt used. As a grown woman, she could never trust the men who wanted to be with her. She felt that they, like her parents, just wanted to be with her because her beauty made them look good. She became very negligent of her body, as if to test people's affection, and eventually this self-neglect developed into a serious physical condition for which she had to be hospitalised.

To change a negative attitude you might have about your body, you need to replace what has been learned and stored in your old brain with self-loving beliefs. Following that, then you can go and act with this new positive image of yourself.

PATTERN AWARENESS

Can you remember any messages you might have heard from your parents and family about the body? They might have been 'casual' comments, but they registered in your brain. Some examples could be:

- So-and-so is so fat
- You'll only get a husband if . . .
- You look like a slut
- Oh no, I've put on so much weight
- She's really let herself go, hasn't she?
- I don't care if you're not hungry. Eat it up
- You've been so good. Here's some chocolate for you

What effect have these messages had on your life? 'You look like a slut' might have shut the door on your own femininity or burgeoning sexuality. 'Eat it up' – whether hungry or not – could have led you to lose touch with your natural appetite. 'Here's some chocolate for you' could have led to comfort eating. Do the elevator exercise (see page 117) if you need more information on what you picked up when a child.

After that, as you got older, what messages did you learn as a teenager, when most of us really wanted to be accepted by our peer group? 'That is so uncool' could have left you terrified of looking different or 'wrong'. One of the most common nightmares is to dream we arrive at school wearing the wrong things and are the object of laughter. We may have been creating pressure on ourselves for years because we still fear being laughed at. We'll wear things that are really uncomfortable or plain impractical rather than suffer *that* fate.

When you look around you now as an adult, are you still listening to the myth of the right body and looks? You may well have lost your own voice along the way.

The body finds a voice

Having discovered the messages that give us a negative image, the next step is to see if we can loosen some of these old beliefs through expression. Your body doesn't often get to speak up; it usually has to put up with whatever's going on. So just *imagine* that your body could have a voice and was going to use that voice to speak up against the Intellect and Emotions. They, after all, have been making your body suffer while they run around in conflict and disharmony, as you saw in Chapter Seven. Go ahead and say whatever it is that you need to say to them. Together, the Intellect and Emotions are called, simply, Mind. Your dialogue might go something like this:

Body (with energy): You work me too hard. You never let me rest. And, you tell me I'm too old and fat and wrinkly.

Mind (scornfully): For goodness sake, look after yourself for a change. Stop complaining.

Body: I'm trying to tell you what's going on inside. The only way to get you to shut up these days is to give you a headache!

Mind: Well, what is it that you're trying to tell me?

Body: Please don't work so hard. Stop sitting at your computer and get out more!

Mind: And lose my job?

Body: I'm not saying you'll get fired. I'm suggesting you reach a balance. I need to rest and relax. Because of the workload, I even find it hard to sleep. You haven't been switching off recently, have you?

So far they have been focusing on the problem. After a while, you'll find that it seems natural to look for a solution.

Mind: No, that's true. I've been running at top speed for too long. Do you have some ideas for what we might do?

Body: Yes, I do. I want you to take longer weekends, and not to bring your work back home. I also would like you to do some outdoor things with your friends and colleagues. Not just sit around in restaurants and bars.

Mind: Like what, play tennis?

Body: Sure. How about we invite them to play a game, or perhaps a round of golf?

Mind: Hey, those are good ideas. I'm not too sure about golf – it's been so long. But tennis, we could knock a ball around I guess.

Body: When?

Mind: I'll talk to Nick first and see if he can make Tuesday next week.

WORKING IT OUT

What do *your* body and mind need to let out? What's often the struggle or underlying conflict between them? Does your body need to mention too much work and not enough exercise? Is it the conflict with the body's ill-health or lack of energy versus the mind's need to gather information? Does your mind feel let down by your body's restlessness or aches? Whatever it is, let them voice their frustrations until they each feel they have had their say. Then look at what they could agree on. Don't let it be a compromise that both sides would find less than satisfactory and later resent. When they have agreed on something, straightaway get the two of them to write out a contract before they forget what it is. Make them decide on *specific* actions at *specific* times, not something as vague as, 'Let's try and get out more.' Vague plans have a habit of disappearing into a mysterious black hole. Start getting specific right now, for example:

Mind: I agree to (stop work at 6 pm, not pick up my voice mail on the weekends, arrange times to play tennis)

_____

_____

_____

Body: I agree to (eat organic food three times a week, go dancing on Thursday evenings, go to sleep earlier).

_____

Keep adding generously to your contract between the body and the mind. Find things either that both enjoy, or that they each will have a turn at choosing. For example, 'I agree that you can read the Sunday papers if you agree that we go for a good long walk at one of my favourite places afterwards.' Stick the contract somewhere where you can easily be reminded of it, like on the fridge door. Then, most importantly, act on your promises!

Get into action

What are *you* prepared to do for your body? When was the last time you danced? Isn't it about time you really moved your energy? Get some music on your stereo or go out to a club. Dance like no one's watching! Have you been sitting around munching junk food in front of the TV? Throw the junk food into the bin, turn off the TV and head out the door. Hire some in-line skates or get out on your bicycle.

What could you do that your body would so associate with fun and feeling good that it might just develop a healthy addiction? If we're all addicts, better that we find healthy rather than harmful habits to indulge!

Delight in the flow of energy. Move yourself! Now!

PRACTICAL EXERCISES
TO HELP YOU ACCEPT YOUR BODY

In order to feel more comfortable with your body, you might have to work on self-acceptance. Including this aspect of your Quadrinity sometimes gets forgotten, but is so important for both giving and receiving love. Use this exercise to develop more loving self-acceptance.

Self-acceptance

Go to a mirror and look at your eyes for at least one minute. Look at your eyes with love and acceptance. Go deep into them and stay with them long enough to go beyond self-consciousness. Look at your eyes as if you were looking at someone you had just fallen in love with.

Next, with that same feeling of love, look at your own face. See your nose, cheeks, lips, chin, jaw, ears with a feeling of acceptance and admiration. Breathe in that sense of emotional goodness. Touch your face to feel how soft it is. Wonder at how it has carried you through all the years of your life's experience.

Now, leaving the mirror, get into a comfortable position either sitting or lying down. Sense your rhythm of breathing and imagine breathing in a loving, golden light through the crown of your head. As you breathe out, imagine breathing out any negative messages and any old darkness inside of your body through your navel. Breathing in, let this golden light spread down through your face and eyes. Then it goes down your neck and shoulders, into your chest, warming and softening you.

The golden light now touches your heart centre, filling you with an abundance of love. It spreads from there down to your navel. Feel it softening you. Let the warmth of goodness now spread out through your arms and legs to the tips of your fingers and toes. Your entire body is suffused with love and acceptance. Remember to breathe out the old energy of fear, pain and shame. Let go any remaining sense of anger and vindictiveness anywhere in your body. Let it be replaced by love.

Stay with this for a few minutes until you feel total acceptance of your body.

A shorter exercise, one that does not require you to be alone, is to get a photo of yourself, a close-up showing your body shape. Carry it around with you, or put it up somewhere prominent in your home. Whenever you look at this photo, do so with conscious acceptance and love. Affirm to yourself some positive messages about your body as you look at the photo. If a part of your mind has reservations when you say 'I love my body', overpower it with your love.

Enjoying a closer relationship with the body

There are times to move and times to be still. After you have shifted your energy, sit for a few moments just noticing your body. Scan all the way through from head to toe as if you had a radar attached to one hand. Pass one hand down very slowly, putting your attention on where your hand is.

How do you feel as you are doing this? Are you enjoying the flow of energy that you have become aware of? Can you let yourself take even more delight in your body?

What insight about your physical welfare are you receiving as you do this scan? Is your body giving you signals that you need to pay attention to some part in particular? Any signals you receive can be taken as healthy reminders of what you need to do more or, perhaps, less of.

THE SENSUAL WORLD OF THE BODY

The body is the doorway to the rich world of the senses. We can explore them all far more.

Delight in the body's sense of taste. What you eat can give you energy or, just as easily, can drain you. Prepare your own food with love and care. When you eat a meal, do it with mindfulness. Know you are doing this to return something to your physical self. Eating healthy food, you are more likely to retain your positive energy and avoid stuck feelings that lead to depression. If your energy starts dropping off, eat a slow-burning, natural source of glucose rather than the quick hit of a chocolate bar. Listen to what your body needs. While some of us need plenty of carbohydrates, others are better off with salads and vegetables.

Get out into the fresh air, especially if you have a desk-bound job. When you are outside, look around and notice what's there. Delight your sense of sight with the rich colours of nature. Delight in the body's sense of smell with the scents around you – the grass, or flowers, the smell of the rain on the damp earth.

Take delight in the body's sense of touch. Do you have regular massage? Nurturing touch is important for the welfare of your body. If you are in a relationship, do you touch each other regularly with care and attention?

With music, take delight in the body's sense of hearing. Hear the songs of the birds. On the next windy day, listen to the wind through the trees. See if you can find a difference in sound between the different trees.

Your body can give you so much pleasure. Enjoy its rich sensual world as you learn more and more about its own wisdom.

Remember that your body enables you to express yourself emotionally. Your voice, arms, legs, and whole physical being are there for you to get those feelings out. Intellectually, your body houses the brain. If you feel stressed or are tired, your intellect will underperform. Spiritually, your body is the channel between the human and the divine. Your eyes alone reflect that. Sparkling, clear eyes show life's energy running through you. As the 'windows of the soul', they can also express a deep love where no words are necessary. When you allow true eye contact, you are letting someone in to see you. That's true intimacy.

You are mind-body-spirit, all in one. One of the main goals of this process of change is to return back to the knowledge that we are loveable, just as we are. All parts of us equally deserve to be loved and accepted unconditionally. From your own cup of love, start by loving your body. That sense of emotional goodness will then spread out to include the other aspects of your being. You become certain of the fact that you are loved and that you are a loving person. When you then pass this feeling and this energy on to others in your life, your whole world becomes a richer and more fulfilling place. You have found your loving home, *now* in the present moment and *here* in your body.

15

Celebrating Your Sexuality

*I'd like to meet the person who invented sex and
see what they're working on now.*

ANONYMOUS

Sex is a wonderful way to explore the body and feel the pleasure
it can give you and others. It channels the physical expression
of our love for each other. It's the doorway to the rich world
of the senses. It's natural, vital and full of wonderful energy.

Sex is one of the last remaining primeval forces still in our
bodies. It cannot be 'civilised', though it can be sublimated.
Unpredictable as it is, it has been scorned or repressed by many
a religion. It simply has too much energy attached to it. So sex
either gets ignored or actively discouraged. Society also tries
to control our sexuality, but this life-affirming force is not
easily controlled.

Used well and without judgement, our bodies love the full
aliveness and orgasmic potential of our sexuality. But there
are many deeply entrenched patterns associated with sex that
people would prefer are never, ever brought into the open.
Often there is no middle ground around sex, and we are
left with strong opposites. It is either an obsession or
repressed.

Harry had spent his life in the pursuit of women. As a musician on the road for months at a time, he had many opportunities for a casual relationship, most of them lasting just as long as his band was in town. When he finally stopped travelling and moved in with his lover, he found it very hard not to keep thinking about who would be his next conquest. Every time he went out, whether it was to a party, a walk in the park, or simply a meal in a restaurant, his eyes checked out who was available. After many years, he was adept at recognising the signals that women sent out. He always knew when to make his move. Harry fits the classic profile of a sex addict, needing a 'fix' even though sex outside of his relationship put that partnership at great risk. He said he really could not help himself. He had to have a fresh 'supply' for his addiction, and the greater the risk of being found out, the more exciting he found it.

Myrna would be called a 'sexual anorexic'; by the time she was twenty-eight, she had only had sex four times, with two different lovers. She was in love with her partners at the time, and both times she had been dumped soon after. Her heart had been broken, and so she swore she would never allow herself to be hurt that way again. She channelled all her creativity into her publishing career, but was unhappy because she felt that a relationship was more important than work. She longed to have a family.

Harry was cut off from his heart, Myrna from her sexuality. One obsessed over sex, the other repressed it. They both lost out. If only they could connect sex with heart, their sexuality would be a wonderful way to celebrate their bodies in love with someone else.

How about you? Are you comfortable with yourself as a sexual being? Is it OK to feel yourself as someone who has natural sexual desires? Do you value your sexuality as a part of your whole being? Or is it something you feel is in the way of your life, your personal development, and especially of your spirituality? Is it possible for you to consider sex as *sacred*?

What would you like to make your sex life even better? More fun, more orgasms, more often? A partner, maybe! If you love your body, and feel good about it – even if it's different from what the media considers beautiful – you will naturally be able to enjoy sex far more.

Take an inventory of your sex life today. When you last made love, what was it like? Did you have a full body orgasm? Did you allow yourself the pleasure? Were you happy with what happened between you and your partner? In general, do you talk about what it is that you both like? What do you do to set the scene for sex? Do you still have spontaneous sex rather than feeling it's become part of a routine?

What is it that you would like to change about your sex life now?

Our attitudes to sex

Knowing what you want is a great start to making positive changes. By now, I'm sure you know, though, what needs to be done before you can get there. We need to look at the influence of the past.

Do you remember how you *first* learned about sex? I most certainly do. As a twelve-year-old, I was handed a well-thumbed book one day at school. An elder boy gave it to me with a knowing grin. It was called *The Life and Loves of Frank Harris*, and detailed the various conquests of a Victorian serial seducer. I could not believe what I was reading! Here it was, the act, the deed that had such mystery attached to it. The stuff of many a whispered conversations among us boys. It was very exciting – my body didn't lie on that point – and all the more so because it felt like a forbidden subject. The big leap I had to make was this: could my parents ever have really done *that*? The author left nothing to the imagination as he wandered the bedrooms of Victorian England and France. This act of sex felt so clandestine, so illegal, and I knew my parents to be law-abiding people. This was all very confusing.

I had not been told *anything* about sex up to that point by my teachers or parents. There was a big gap between how important it seemed to us and how little we had heard about it from our elders. What were we to imagine if they had left out this part of our education? That it didn't matter? Judging by how our bodies were reacting with hormones charging around, it did matter. But it seemed separate from the lives of adults, as if it existed on another level of reality.

Was this how it was for you when you were growing up before the onset of your own puberty? For many people sex somehow exists on this different level of reality to regular life. And not only because of what was not said about it.

For you to have a healthy attitude towards sex, be fully aware of what you were taught about it when you were growing up. Or perhaps this should be phrased the other way around. Be aware of what you *weren't* taught about sex when you were growing up. Remember, the unspoken messages can have as much or even more power than the actual spoken messages.

Did you hear any of these messages when you were a child?

- Sex is dirty
- Sex is your duty
- Sex is for using or manipulating someone
- Sex is how to win a man/woman
- Sex is a performance
- Sex is disgusting
- Sex is something to be endured on a Saturday night after a few drinks
- Sex is expected
- Sex gets you into trouble
- Sex will get you pregnant

- Sex is for trapping someone into marriage
- Sex is only acceptable after you are married
- Sex will give you a bad reputation
- Sex is a weapon
- Sex is not to be spoken about because it is shameful
- Sex is better when watching porn
- Sex is not enjoyable for women
- Sex proves you are a man
- Sex means jealousy

If you acknowledge that some of these messages became lodged inside of you, what *now* goes on in your head when you make love? Think back over your recent sexual history. Could you fully enter into love-making, or did you hold back in some way? Did you use sex as a reward, or to punish your partner? Did you need pornography or to fantasise about someone else in order to get turned on? Were you worried about your performance? Did you find it easy to communicate your wishes, or were you too embarrassed?

What is it that you need to change?

HOW TO CHANGE OUR ATTITUDES TO SEX

If it's hard for us to accept any aspect of our own fully alive sexuality, we need to get a good grip on the roots of that conditioning and tear them out.

If you want to uproot those patterns and beliefs, you are going to have to walk back into the past and take a good look at what was being modelled and what was being said. Did your parents touch and cuddle each other, showing you that physical intimacy was normal between people who loved each other? Did you get the sense that they enjoyed their own sensuality by the way they moved? When you were at school, what did you learn?

What is your attitude to sex and intimacy now? Look at this list and be honest with yourself. Are any of these patterns true for you? Remember, to undo any blocks first we have to know what they might be made up of.

Patterns around sex:

- [ ] Rejects intimacy, touching, hugging, or kissing
- [ ] Avoids sex
- [ ] Sexually passive/disinterested
- [ ] Unworthy of pleasure
- [ ] Premature ejaculation
- [ ] Non-orgasmic
- [ ] Lack of spontaneity/creativity
- [ ] Don't get what I want
- [ ] Cannot ask for what I want
- [ ] Prudish/puritanical
- [ ] Fear of sexual performance
- [ ] Fear of intimacy
- [ ] Fear of masturbation/sex
- [ ] Must/can't fantasise
- [ ] Excessive masturbation/sex
- [ ] Promiscuity/affairs
- [ ] Prostitution/visit prostitutes
- [ ] Sexually provocative/seductive
- [ ] Manipulates through sex
- [ ] Dominates through sex
- [ ] Sexually abusive/violent
- [ ] Rape (victim or abuser)

☐ Child sexual molestation/incest
☐ Ignores sexual molestation/incest
☐ Invalidates sexuality
☐ Invalidates sexual orientation
☐ Fear of homosexuality/bisexuality

Beliefs about sex:

☐ Nice girls don't do it/enjoy it
☐ Love them and leave them
☐ Fake it to please your man
☐ Men are only after one thing
☐ Never trust men/women
☐ Smart women aren't sexy
☐ It's not OK to be sexy

Once you have done an honest inventory of your own patterns, trace any patterns that ring true back to the past. Go over the list once more and consider which of these patterns and beliefs you might have picked up as an impressionable child. It may be helpful also to identify which parent, or surrogate parent, such as a teacher, had that pattern or passed on that belief to you. Make it clear through tracing back that you *learned* them, so that you can give yourself the possibility of learning and believing something different.

When you are aware of some of the limiting patterns, either on paper or in your mind, the next step is to disidentify from them. Don't do this simply as an intellectual exercise, else it will be dry and meaningless. You won't remember it either emotionally *or* in your body. Do it with the feeling that you deserve a rich and sensual experience of sex. Imagine the huge pleasure that would give you!

One simple and effective way of dis-identification you know well already. You can write a letter, first expressing the damage the patterns have done to you. Then you 'give them back'. You can make this exercise far more powerful by specifically listing the times in your life when you have felt sexually repressed or confused, needy or desperate, and be clear that it's over, that you have had enough. Hand back your negative sexual history.

When you have done that, follow the other steps towards change:

Expression: As you know, insights and awareness are good, but not enough to change your behaviour. If you have written down the most damaging messages you ever heard about sex on a piece of paper, you have expressed them. To see them gone, tear the letter up, or better still, burn it. Scatter the ashes to the wind and make a vow to yourself to change. If you don't feel like writing them, express them by shouting or having a dialogue where your body gets to speak how it feels about sexual patterns.

Forgiveness: If there are incidents concerning sex in your life that you are ashamed about, speak those into the fire (see Chapter Eight). Let go of the darkness you have held inside. Let the past be in the past so that you can move ahead. Forgive yourself. If it's not harmful to do so, ask for forgiveness from anyone whom you might have hurt.

New Behaviour: Now you can go ahead and make those changes a reality. Explore your sexual side. Take delight in your sexuality. You are a creative being, and a true creative act is to make love. Used as a healthy expression of our alive sensual bodies, sex is a wonderful way to make a bridge between the physical and the spiritual realms. It really can be sacred. If you don't have a partner, put on some slow music and dance in the most sensual way you can. Be present to the wonder of yourself as a sexual being.

Our childlike nature really loves sex. It's fun, exciting, energetic and gives us a lot of pleasure. We love spontaneity and change. You wouldn't expect a child to play hide-and-seek in the same way every time. Similarly, you wouldn't want to make love in the same way every time. Experiment with different places, different times, different positions, even different things to wear. As for the Intellect, well, our Intellect doesn't need a big part in sex. In fact, our Intellects have a habit of interfering in the simple pleasures, and have been known to sabotage orgasms. If you have a particularly over-active mind, imagine leaving it outside the door. Tell it that it can't come in until you have finished!

You do not have to be making love to enjoy the *sensual* side of your being. A wonderful exercise, which you can do by yourself or with a partner, is to take a warm bath. The warm water relaxes you, calms your mind and brings you back into your body. Candles spread around the bathtub cast a warm glow to soften the mood. If they are scented, the candles can add to the whole experience by delighting the sense of smell. Now let yourself touch and, if you are there with a partner, be touched . . .

The miracle of the sexual, sensual body

Accepting and loving our bodies as sexual and sensual means that we have integrated the fourth aspect of our Quadrinity to take its place along with our spiritual, emotional and intellectual aspects. A major goal of this process of change is to be self-loving, and this of course includes our bodies. But as well as that, now we can express love physically through our bodies free of patterns – we can give as well as receive love.

While the body guides us into the physical world with its myriad of delightful sensations, sex itself provides an immediate way of channelling one of our strongest life energies. It reminds us to take risks, to be open to new experiences, and to be loving beings. It connects the spiritual world of unconditional love with the earthly world of physical love.

You can now let yourself be fully present to life by feeling and enjoying your body at every moment. Remember, just as you are, you are loveable. You deserve this life, rich with a vast array of experiences.

16

The Courage to Change

*One of the things I learnt when I was negotiating was that until I
changed myself, I could not change others.*

NELSON MANDELA

Working through this book, you have now gone through a
powerful process of change. Congratulations! Your life is ready
for a rich new direction.

The Process of this book now becomes *your* Process. You are
on a journey, a dynamic movement of perpetual change. You
have learned to shake off the past and free up your energy.
Your conscious awareness of yourself and your environment is
now much greater. The exciting part is using that heightened
awareness on your own positive and ongoing flow of change.

THE RIVER OF LIFE

Imagine that life is a river, and you're in a small boat going
with the flow of the current. Every moment as the water swirls
around you is a different one.

The river at times is straight, and you can see far ahead
into the future. At other times there are many bends, and life

changes quickly without warning. Some of the days you paddle along in quiet, calm water, while other days are full of rough stretches. The river would not be as exciting without the rough water in the rapids. In the rapids, you have to use your skills to keep your balance. It is sometimes all you can do to stay in your boat. Your attention is completely in the moment.

As Don Juan, the Yaqui shaman, said to Carlos Castaneda: 'To the normal person, everything is either a blessing or a curse. To the warrior, everything is a challenge.'

You have come a long way already. Life, with all its rough patches and calm periods, is a series of challenges making you learn and grow.

With every day that passes, you gain more experience in how to handle your boat. You learn how to read the currents and see where is safe. There is power around you and a sense of responsibility. You have a paddle in your hands for balance and direction. You know how to live life. You know how to love.

Doing the Process in this book, you have come a long way on your journey in life. You have found a powerful way to undo the lessons of the past. You have discarded damaging patterns of behaviour and learned new ways of being. You have discovered a love for yourself and others that had always been there. Share that love with yourself, with others, and with the world that we all live in.

A BEAUTIFUL FUTURE

Remember the vision you created back in Chapter Three for your life in general, as well as in Chapter Eleven for your work? What do you want for your future? Look at it. Think big. Dream big. Consider what your heart desires, not what you think is possible. Remember, there are four areas to contemplate in your vision:

- Self
- Relationships
- Home
- Work

Keep fine-tuning this vision. You can add to it or take away at any time. I took a yacht out of my vision when I realised it might require too much time! Though I love to be able to travel, I'm better with things that are simple, cannot break down and are easy to move. I replaced the yacht with a kayak.

You have probably imagined all kinds of changes while reading this book. You are motivated to start now because you truly want your relationship to be more open and trusting, your work to be more meaningful and rewarding, and your connection to yourself to be more authentic.

As we all know, *imagining* change is great, but *acting* to change things is far better. For us to put our ideas into action, we need an ongoing discipline to remind us on a daily, weekly and yearly level.

Let's look at some disciplines that can keep us on the path of positive change.

YOUR PROCESS IN ACTION

Daily plan:
- Every day, spend some time alone. Let thoughts go, even if it's when you're in your car looking at the traffic lights.
- Every day, think of what you have to be grateful for. Express your appreciation in some way.

- Every day, make contact with someone in a way that goes deeper than the normal 'How are you?' level. Give them a hug if it feels appropriate. Share your feelings with them (and not just the negative ones, even though most people believe that misery loves company). Share your experiences of life with them, and find yourself becoming closer to them, as well as closer to your own experiences.

- Every day, check in with your Quadrinity. Scan your feelings, thoughts, body sensations and spiritual connection. Ask yourself the simple questions: What am I feeling right now? What am I thinking right now? What is my body telling me? What is my spiritual self saying? See if there is balance between them, or which part needs special attention.

- Buy yourself a notebook and use it to write down your impressions of the day. You might be writing about yourself, other people, your surroundings, or your hopes and dreams. If you write at least three pages you'll get a good flow going and reach beneath self-consciousness.

Weekly plan:
- How many days in the week have you managed those daily tasks? Where do you feel satisfied, where do you feel unsatisfied?
- Ask yourself the following questions. Choose to do them at the same time on the same day each week. It's best on the day that signifies for you the end of the week. I always choose a late Sunday afternoon, when there's usually a feeling of 'winding down' from the last seven days.

What have I done for my body this week?
What have I done for my creative, childlike Emotional self this week?
What have I done for my curious Intellect this week?
What have I done for my Spiritual self this week?

Remember, you are your own best teacher. If you are asking yourself questions, you're already well on the way to finding out the answers that you need to hear.

Yearly plan:
- Once a year, give yourself a holiday. Let it be a true vacation. Not a time when you fill yourself up with new experiences, but a time when you empty yourself. 'Vacation' comes from the Latin word for 'empty'. Take some of your vacation time to lessen the input, reduce the stimulation. Go off on a retreat. It doesn't have to be at a dedicated retreat centre (though if you go to one, they will of course respect your space and need for quietness). You can have your own retreat in any style you wish. It could be at a five star hotel if you would prefer to associate retreat with comfort. Or take a tent into a beautiful natural setting.
- There, look back on the year and see how far you have come. Own and integrate the lessons of the past twelve months. Forgive yourself for mistakes you might have made. Appreciate the positive changes you have initiated.
- Celebrate the passing of one year with a ritual of your own devising. A friend of mine who loves rituals around fire, burned all the journals she had written in the past year. If you love to keep mementoes and find it hard

to give things up, you might still do something symbolic like taking a page or an article of clothing or a photo and offering it up for 'sacrifice'. Some say that this is a natural law: you have to give something up to gain something in return. On the other hand, you might feel better collecting photos and images of the past year and making a collage of them.

Some facts about the process of change

You will get encouragement from sources you had no idea existed. You will learn that help is always available. You will get wake-up calls to prevent you from dozing off. You will find yourself with kindred spirits. Like you, they love new challenges. Like you, they are excited by learning new ways. They will become your new travel companions.

Once in a while you will need to rest. It's totally normal. Accept that this path of change is more demanding than staying in our comfort zone. Take time for yourself and don't be frightened to let your friends know that you need this time.

If you try denying the need for time out, it'll shout even louder in your ear.

Own your experience

When you accept certain emotions and experiences, rather than rejecting them as bad or unnecessary, your process can deepen. I remember the relief I felt when, instead of rejecting depression, I *allowed* myself to feel depressed. I indulged in it, and threw in a dose of self-pity for good measure. Then I sat back and looked at its effect on me. 'Hmmm,' I thought. 'This depression is really rather interesting. It's another way the mind-body-spirit works. Perhaps it's all grist for the mill rather than an empty, grey mood of mine.' I came out of it soon after, with renewed energy. The depression had been a way of making me shut down and rest for a while.

You can try the same thing with boredom, anxiety, shame, guilt, anger, or indeed any thought or feeling you might experience during the day. Firstly, heighten the awareness of yourself and then exaggerate it until it passes, moves on to another thought or feeling, or is resolved within you. It has been there for a reason.

The next time you have a feeling or a thought that you find uncomfortable, rather than rejecting it, own it as part of your experience and see what you can learn from it. That way you can integrate it into a more whole you.

Trust that you will find the best way of dealing with things.

The strength of support

It's no accident that twelve-step groups, such as Alcoholics Anonymous, Overeaters Anonmyous and Codependents Anonymous, have grown so exponentially in the last fifty years. They answer a basic need we all have, which is to find support among kindred spirits.

One of the great modern paradoxes is that we now have so many ways to communicate with each other, yet we feel more and more isolated. We yearn for contact. And rightly so. A healthy community around us is as valuable as a myriad of powerful techniques. The community reminds us of what we have learned and how far we have come. We see the challenges ahead, and are encouraged by others to stay on the path. When we falter, they are there to support us. When we are strong and others lose heart, we are there to support them.

Share your hopes and dreams with five friends. Why five? So that at any time someone might be thinking of you, and you might be thinking of them. It gets the intention out there. If you're witnessed you're more likely to put things into action.

Who are the people around you that you would like to include on your journey? Visualise them coming along hand in hand on this path of discovery. Some may be faster, some slower, but they will go down that same road as you.

I encourage you to form your own group with others who share your goals. It may be that you are a group of artists and wish to support each others' creativity. A side-effect might be that you teach each other the self-confidence to sell your art in the world. You may be a group who have met in a large corporation, and realise that you all need to get out and play more. Instead of going to the pub or bar after work, you meet up for a 'play support group' – you might have to call it something different, like a football club or baseball league, so that your play time gets approval from your more serious intellect!

You will find your kindred spirits. These people, committed to growing, will keep you on the right path even more than a polished and practised set of techniques. Call people up more. Drop in on them. Find an excuse to meet. As you continue on your path, you will discover that there is a magnetic field around you that attracts people of a similar spirit.

Remember, ultimately, you have the wisdom, love and strength within to carry you through life's journey. Whatever help you may get along the way, the lessons you experience are your greatest teaching.

It's your Process now. Live it fully and you will truly have a future very different from your past.

APPENDIX A

The Hoffman toolbox

The four essentials:
- Awareness
- Expression
- Forgiveness
- New Behaviour

Awareness:
- Pattern-tracing
- Listing roles
- Elevator
- Emotional self, Intellectual self
- Spiritual self
- Left road, Right road

Expression:
- Letter-writing and letter-burning
- Bashing or stomping
- Vocalising
- Emotions-Intellect dialogue
- Vow to self
- Releasing shame
- Transference communication exercise
- Dancing

Forgiveness:
- Dialogue with parents as a child
- Compassion ritual
- List of mistakes and self-forgiveness
- Candle ritual
- Masterpiece with parents
- Appreciation for self and others

New Behaviour (a thousand and one possibilities!):
- Giving and inviting feedback
- Writing mission statement
- Throwing a birthday party
- Dance sessions
- Rollerblading/cycling/sailing
- Playing with your kids
- Making music
- Singing
- Acting
- Horse-riding
- Parachuting/paragliding
- Samba/salsa lessons
- Diving

Meditations and visualisations:
- Quadrinity check-in
- Visioning
- Sanctuary
- I am that I am
- Seeing your own funeral

Suggested music:
For expression: 'Dynamic Meditation', Osho
For forgiveness: 'Titania' and 'Silverwing', Mike Rowland

For meditations and visualisations:
'Miracles', Robert Whitesides-Woo
'Sojourn', Robert Whitesides-Woo

Anything by:
Tim Wheater
Medwyn Goodall
Deuter
Kitaro
Vangelis

The Hoffman Process residential course and The Hoffman Institute

THE ORIGINS OF THE HOFFMAN PROCESS

Bob Hoffman grew up in New York and moved out to California as an adult. He first started working with people in the radical and turbulent times of the late 1960s. He was acutely aware of the pressing need to create some kind of therapeutic process which might redress all kinds of personal issues. Again and again he saw how people were being prevented from realising and achieving their true potential by the shadows of their past.

He studied with various people to develop his natural intuitive gifts, including Rose Strongin, and then found he was able to do psychic readings for people that proved amazingly accurate.

One of his closest friendships was with a Freudian psychoanalyst and neurologist called Siegfried Fischer. Fischer was much older than him and a mentor for his theories. Together they talked long and profoundly about how we became the way we are. Bob began to understand on a level beyond intellectual comprehension how we developed our personalities.

Although he was not trained as a psychologist, Hoffman possessed an extraordinary gift for intution, which drew many people to him in need of help and guidance. As the success of his work grew, it drew attention from renowned psychiatrists and educators. In 1972, Hoffman, in collaboration with the psychiatrist and psychoanalyst Dr Claudio Naranjo, developed it into a highly effective and cathartic healing programme. Initially the Hoffman Process was conceived as a form of group work, which stretched over thirteen weeks and involved clients coming to regular evening and weekend sessions. It was not until 1985 that Hoffman transformed the process into an intensive residential eight-day seminar, which became known as The Hoffman Quadrinity Process.

For a few years this revolutionary seminar was only available in the USA and Brazil, but in 1987 Hoffman presented his work at a conference for transpersonal psychology in Europe. His ideas were so well received that branches of the Hoffman Institute were soon set up all over Europe. Canada, Australia and Argentina followed shortly afterwards. The Process is now available in fourteen countries throughout the world (see page 280), where select organisations are licensed by Hoffman Institute International to run the eight-day Process in strict accordance with its principles and structure. The Process is facilitated by a highly trained team of teachers, all of whom have been certified in this methodology.

WHAT DOES THE HOFFMAN INSTITUTE DO?

The mission of the Hoffman Institute International is three-fold: to safeguard the standards of the Hoffman Process, foster its growth throughout the world, and participate in the awakening of spiritual consciousness. We focus on raising the personal awareness and self-development of the individual, and through the individual to his or her family and society.

By first helping participants of the Process to become aware of their patterns and character traits, they are able to begin a powerful personal transformation which ends in enabling them to live a far more positive and productive life. These changes are helped and encouraged by a variety of techniques to keep the essential Beingness to the forefront and to stay aligned with all four aspects of the Quadrinity (emotional, mental, physical and spiritual aspects).

How is this done?

The residential Process is carefully designed to enable each person to see how they function both as an individual and as a member of a social group. The experiences of the week automatically throw up different reactions and behaviour patterns. The Process itself is more or less divided into two parts, the first part being a journey of discovery to strip away the layers until the core of the problem is exposed. Once this has been done, the participant begins the second half of the journey, which concentrates on the integration of the Quadrinity and the willingness to accept personal responsibility. During the Process, a variety of techniques and methodologies are used, some of which could be compared to Gestalt Therapy, Bioenergetics or Family Systems Theory, and include methods such as individual sessions, visualisation, externalisation of emotions, autobiographical writing and educational presentations. It is the combination or the menu that makes the Process so challenging, cathartic and immensely healing.

The Hoffman Process cannot be easily defined, categorised or compared with other kinds of therapy or counselling purely because it has a completely unique approach to personal development. It is often said by people in the healing profession that the eight days of the residential course are perhaps equal to two or more years of therapy. Its effectiveness lies in it being an intensive residential experience which uses a combination of techniques to create a clearly structured and logical path for self-discovery. It has been found effective for men and women from all walks of life, whether they are new to personal development, or have had years of experience.

Consider the 'highs' given by a new relationship, a bar of chocolate, a glass of champagne or by making a killing on the stock market. If we could take that kind of chemical release and associate it with a healthy behaviour, such as communicating honestly, or going for a walk in the hills around our home, then we are far more likely to continue that behaviour. The Hoffman Process aims to lead people into making new associations through a form of deep emotional education, not by merely talking it through. These new associations go beyond being chemically based, though I have heard many talk of their new 'natural highs'. They feel far more fulfilled because they also satisfy a more profound aspect of ourselves, that which lies underneath. Gandhi called it the 'still, small voice within', the voice of our essential 'being-ness' or 'essence'.

In a faster-paced world, though, we need almost to trick ourselves into attaining that sense of inner peace. We need to use our brains and their chemicals to return to a place of deeper truth. I believe this is why adventure holidays are so popular now. We all need an active adventure to enjoy nature and solitude to counteract our noisy minds and their need to be busy. We need a really good excuse to go and spend time in the quieter world and listen to ourselves again. So it is with the Hoffman Process; it lets us enjoy an adventure that is exciting as well as challenging. Like a white-water ride, the memories and images associated with the week can remain with us for a lifetime.

There are a lot of therapies available, but they don't take it to the same depths, are not as thorough and all encompassing as the Hoffman Process. I was very impressed with the way they were able to incorporate so many aspects of the therapeutic process into one whole system and get the depth they did. Others go so far, but they don't take it to the end. I have continued using the techniques and continue to benefit from them.

Sister Ambrose Stachine,
Provincial Superior for the Sister Servants of Mary Immaculate, Canada

TAKING TIME FOR OURSELVES

It is not often that we give ourselves time to be who we are. Indeed most of us are so afraid of who we are that we take every opportunity to avoid ourselves. Consequently we find ourselves on a daily hamster wheel of commuting to jobs that we do not find fulfilling, in which we are met by absurd deadlines, telephones, e-mails, computer screens and a round of meetings. When we get home it's time to look after others but not ourselves, fit in some shopping before collapsing in front of the television with a drink in hand. All this leads to self-isolation, and then we wonder why we have poor relationships.

When the Hoffman Process is run as a residential course it gives people an opportunity to *stop* their world (an expression Don Juan used with Castaneda) and to clamber off their frenetic hamster wheel. It also provides protection, a space which is truly safe and sacred, and removes the mundane work and household roles which could take the focus away from what is being faced in that moment. These eight days are therefore a precious gift – a period of time which participants dedicate to themselves and to themselves alone, probably for the first time in their lives. In addition it allows the time for important flashes of intuition, insights and inspiration to gestate. A gleaning of understanding on the first day might not be fully understood until the last day. People are therefore invited not to make contact with family, friends or work colleagues, once again in order to keep the focus from possibly being taken away from what they are facing within themselves. This of course can throw up challenges. However, because of the intensity of the Process, within a very short space of time it becomes abundantly clear how important it is to respect a personal need for privacy.

The eight days are very intensive. This is not a course where you can show up at ten o'clock after a leisurely breakfast. The course begins early in the morning and goes on well into the evening. The team of facilitators are always there to help people through any barriers that might come up, and to offer a supporting hand if they feel that they can't take another step.

WHAT KIND OF PERSON COMES ON A PROCESS?

Some people are recommended through friends or family members who have been through the Process and thought it would be a good idea if they went too. Others come recommended by their therapist, counsellor or even business adviser. Many simply open a magazine, read an article or an advertisement and get the feeling deep inside that this is something they have to do – they 'know'. Their intuition leads them to it. Their trust in the Process is also touching. Most come without an inkling of what is going to happen, or indeed wanting to, because they instinctively know this is the start of a longed-for change in their lives. Some are housewives, teachers, priests and carers; others are industrial moguls, rock musicians, politicians and psychiatrists. The ages range from late teens right into the eighties. A few have a clearly defined diagnosis related to issues of self-worth, depression, or addictive-compulsive behaviour, while others are primarily concerned with their personal growth and wish to gain a deeper understanding of themselves.

Each group that gathers on the first day of a residential Hoffman Process is a colourful pot pourri of personalities, age groups and life experiences, all of whom have made the conscious choice to be there. And so the journey of adventure can begin.

WHAT THE GROUP DYNAMIC CAN OFFER

As humans we need social integration to feel included and accepted. The group carries an energy which is healing in its own right as well as providing a safe and supportive environment for people to discover their personal healing. While the Hoffman Process provides the space for this healing to happen, each group creates its own energetic transformation which is quite miraculous.

There's a group synergy and participants can look at other people going through experiences and it gives them some energy and willingness and inspiration to stay the course in their Process.

Mary Nurrie Stearns, Editor of *Personal Transformation* magazine

Of course to some, joining a group of unknown people, no matter what has brought them together, can be challenging in itself. Most of us live in environments where we choose who we mix with. Suddenly finding yourself as part of a group of strangers on the first day can bring up issues such as comparison, shame, self-consciousness or needing to perform and look good. Entrusting yourself to the Process means that you have to let go for the next eight days from doing life 'your way' and that means that your comfortable daily routines will be disrupted. It may be frightening or intimidating to form new relationships with people who perhaps you would not encounter in your ordinary life. As we have already said, all kinds of people are drawn to the Process, and becoming part of such a group may not only bring up but also exaggerate the patterns, judgements and left-over issues that we all carry at some level.

For the first day or two, some people find it quite challenging to settle into the course. However, the group dynamic gathers a momentum of its own, and as each person begins to shed their mask or 'false self', incredibly intense and loving relationships are formed that can last a lifetime. It's like catching a wave because there is a moment when the energy of the group suddenly merges into a magical flow which carries each person along towards their own healing experience. By the end of the week people are able to look back and laugh at the negative reactions they had towards each other when they first met.

The Hoffman Institute strongly recommends that you do the childhood work in your native language. This means reaching back into the emotional memories of your formative period, writing the letters and talking to your internalised parents and inner emotional self in that language. It may be that you have moved countries and not used your native tongue for twenty, thirty years or more. You feel much more articulate and comfortable in your adopted language. No matter. Your mother tongue still remains the language of your dreams and your behaviour as a child. It has much more emotional impact. If it is possible to do the Hoffman Process in the country you grew up in, all the better. You may have an aversion to it. Going back there is all part of the healing journey for 'the only way out is through'.

If you wish to learn more about the residential Hoffman Process, please contact the centre nearest you through the International website, www.hoffmaninstitute.com or from the address list see over page:

HOFFMAN CENTRES

- **United Kingdom**
  Hoffman Institute UK
  Phone: 01903-88-99-90
  Fax: 01903-88-99-91
  Freephone: 0800-068-7114
  Email: info@hoffmaninstitute.co.uk
  www.hoffmaninstitute.co.uk

- **United States**
  Hoffman Institute USA
  Phone: +1-415-485-5220
  Toll Free: 800-506-5253
  Fax: +1-415-485-5539
  Email: hq@hoffmaninstitute.org
  www.hoffmaninstitute.org

- **Australia**
  Hoffman Centre Australia
  Phone: +61-3-9826-2133
  Freecall: 1-800-674-312
  Fax: +61-3-9826-2144
  Email: info@quadrinity.com.au
  www.quadrinity.com.au
  also offered in Malaysia

- **Canada**
  Hoffman Institute Canada
  Phone: +1-519-650-1755
  Toll free: 1-800-741-3449
  Fax: +1-519-650-5590
  Email: info@hoffmaninstitute.ca
  www.hoffmaninstitute.ca

- **Ireland**
  Hoffman Institute Ireland
  Phone: +353-1-820-4422
  Email: ireland@quadrinity.com
  www.quadrinity.com/ireland

- **International Headquarters**
  Hoffman Institute International
  Phone: +1-707-987-2056
  Fax: +1-707-987-3600
  Email: international@quadrinity.com
  www.hoffmaninstitute.com

Rest of the World

- **Argentina**
  Hoffman Institute Argentina
  Phone: +54-11-4833-2567
  Fax: +54-11-4833-2872
  Email: argentina@quadrinity.com
  www.quadrinidad.com.ar

- **Brazil**
  Hoffman Institute Brazil
  Belo Horizonte
  Phone/Fax: +55-31-3223-2037
  Email: hoffman@institutohoffman.com.br
  www.institutohoffman.com.br

  Hoffman Institute – Porto Alegre
  Phone/fax: +55-51-3312-4313
  Email: ihpa@terra.com.br

  Hoffman Institute – Rio de Janeiro
  Phone: +55-21-3816-2400
  Email: rioag@quadrinity.com
  www.institutodevenir.com

Hoffman Institute – Rio de Janeiro
Phone/fax: +55-21-2522-5372
Email: riojsm@quadrinity.com
www.hoffmanrio.hpg.com.br

Hoffman Institute Brazil Sao Paolo
Instituto Thame
Phone/fax: +55-11-3022-7892
Phone/fax: +55-11-3022-9570
Email: insthame@institutothame.com.br
www.institutothame.com.br

- **France**
  Hoffman Institute France
  In France 03-84-20-51-72
  Or phone: +49-761-55-29-66
  Fax: +49-761-56-843
  Email: info@institut-hoffman.com
  www.institut-hoffman.com

- **Germany**
  Berlin: Quadrinity – PTI
  Phone: +49-30-217-66-13
  Fax: +49-30-217-77-19
  Email: quadrinity-berlin@t-online.de
  www.quadrinity.de

  Dusseldorf: Die Lebens Schule
  Tel: +49-700-25-21-00
  Fax: +49-700-25-21-01
  Email: info@lebensschule.de
  www.lebensschule.de

- **Italy**
  Hoffman Institute Italy
  Istituto Wenger
  Tel: +39-02-34-93-83-82
  Fax: +39-02-34-91-266

email: info@quadrinity.it
www.quadrinity.it

- **South Africa**
  Tel: +27-21-853-2737
  Email: info@hoffmaninstitute.co.za
  www.hoffmaninstitute.co.za

- **Spain**
  Hoffman Institute Spain
  Phone/fax: +34-945-27-17-33
  Email: hoffman@euskalnet.net
  www.quadrinity.com/spain

- **Switzerland**
  Hoffman Institute Switzerland
  IAK Institut für Angewandte
  Kurzzeittherapie GmbH
  Phone: +41-81-740-02-84
  Fax: +41-81-740-02-85
  Email: info@iak-quadrinity.ch
  www.iak-quadrinity.ch